Let's Take This Walk of Faith Together!

www.clevelandomcleish.com

The Unshakable Series

FAITH

A THEOLOGICAL MEMOIR

C. ORVILLE MCLEISH

Published by:

ISBN: 978-1-958404-89-8 (paperback)

Dedicated to my "daughter," Chloe, and all the young men and women in our world today who may not yet see their true value and the immeasurable potential they hold within. Despite the challenges you have faced or are facing, remember that your presence here is purposeful; it is no accident. God has imparted a unique greatness inside you that the world eagerly awaits. Embrace every obstacle as an opportunity for growth, for it is through overcoming challenges that you will unlock the limitless potential that lies within you.

This is the book I wish I could make every teenage boy and girl read!

For some reason, I have always been interested in theology. I can absorb depths of knowledge that most Christians I know struggle with.

The point is, it doesn't matter who you are—there is something special about you. If you can find that, you will tap into your greatest potential and begin to live out your purpose.

Every human being is created with unlimited potential, no exceptions. It is up to you to unlock that potential and live out its reality.

PRELUDE

HUMBLE BEGINNINGS

I have not attained the pinnacle of faith seen in the early church and some aspects of our rich Christian history. To date, I have not witnessed the blind see, the deaf hear, the dumb speak, or the dead brought back to life. I have seen and heard tongues and uncontrollable body flinching, but that is about all the spiritual or supernatural phenomena I have experienced with my natural eyes. Of course, I have met people who have seen and even participated in some or all of the above, so I know what is possible.

I realize that faith is a journey, and we cannot skip certain levels to get to the top. We cannot attain heights of faith through political or social manipulation. We cannot bribe our way to the top or somehow cheat the system. Faith is a journey we either choose to take or avoid altogether.

So, why write a memoir titled "Faith?"

To answer this question, you need to know my background and where I am coming from. This way, you will understand that my capacity to own a car and a home, travel the world, earn my Master's degree, get married to a beautiful woman, and write more books than almost every author I know—just to name a few of my accomplishments—is an absolute miracle.

I was born the seventh child to my mother, who had nine children, and the third child to my father, who had two girls before me with his previous wife. I was born out of wedlock and was the first son of my father, who had two more children with my mom after me. I remember my parents' wedding. It took place on a small veranda of our two-bedroom board house. That was my first memory of wearing a suit, and I think I remember it only because the moment was captured on camera.

For the first six years or so of my life, we lived in a rented house. I remember only one night when my father came home drunk. I think he may have been violent at the time as well, but don't quote me on that. I do remember it was a terrible night. Strangely enough, I don't recall most of my childhood, only bits and pieces of it.

I remember when we went to look at this large property with a big "macka" tree in the middle of it. The sun was really hot, and we cooked and ate there under that tree. That was the beginning of our family home, but we were too young to understand the intricacies of that reality. In a short time, a two-bedroom board house was constructed with an enclosed veranda, an outside kitchen, and a pit toilet. It would be many years later before we knew what an inside bathroom with a flushable toilet was. Yes, I grew up with a pit latrine, for those familiar with that. It was home, but as children, we never quite understood, so I never took my friends home from school, even when I went to high school. I was too embarrassed, even though I didn't know that was the reason at the time. I never went to my friends' homes, so I had nothing to compare it with. There was only one friend who ever came to my house, and we called him "Little Man."

I have had a hard and difficult life. I never saw much value or worth in myself. I never believed in myself or put any value at all on who I was. I thought I was just here to survive. What God has done for me in pulling me through the dross of life and making something beautiful of my existence is nothing short of a miracle rooted in a faith I never knew I possessed. I was nothing. A little dark, "fool fool" country boy who was so shy, he could sit in a gym for months watching a girl watching him and never initiate a meaningful conversation. Yet, he got married to one of the most beautiful, smartest, and hardest-working women alive. He moved from being paid a mediocre salary for quality service to starting an unlikely multi-million dollar business, creating a rich, multi-generational legacy not just for himself but for others on a global scale. His name is echoed in many parts of the world, from winning literary awards to seeing his movie and play scripts performed by low and high-budget groups globally, not to mention having books published in English, Spanish, and German.

This is not a testimony of a great man, but of a Great God living inside a man. That reality changes you. I want to speak to those teens and young people who have found an identity only in the prospect of money and sex: life is much bigger than that. Your worth far exceeds silver, gold, and pleasure, but we must first understand our identity by virtue of the finger of our Creator in our lives, the value He puts on us, and the call He has on our lives. We were not sent to earth to be normal. We have a purpose. We have a reason to be here. And though our journey may start in obscurity, God always takes the simplest of things to turn it around to confound the wise. God is not perturbed by our perceived insufficiencies, weaknesses, and struggles because He has always been a God who makes something wonderful out of nothing.

May my journey of faith become fuel for your own journey, allowing God to move you from where you are to where you were created to be. Though the journey may get difficult, I want you to carry on the mantra I have lived my entire life: "Never give up." As my friend, Bishop Valentine Rodney, would often say, "Giving up is not (even) an option."

PREFACE

For years, I have been passionate about one verse of Scripture that I try to intentionally include in all that I do:

"And now abide faith, hope, love, these three; but the greatest of these is love." (1 Corinthians 13:13 - NKJV).

A shaking is coming to the world as we know it. When this happens, only that which is eternal will remain, including you. Everything else that can be shaken will crumble and fall, including every Babylonian system created and established by man.

Taking on the mammoth task of writing about faith was nerve-wracking. I knew that our lives should be built on these three things: ***faith, hope, and love***, but the church I know has never quite mastered any of them. I grew up in a church culture that elevated God but diminished humanity. It meant we were seen as good for nothing, unable or lacking the capacity to do great things. We were taught this lie so early in life that when we became adults and seasoned members of a church, our faith produced very little because it was truncated by everything else that kills faith.

I want to take a journey through the Bible because it speaks of nothing but faith. Interspersed in this journey will be my own faith journey. At first, it was nothing to write home about. I even argued with God that I am not qualified to write on faith with the little experience and manifestations I have seen in my life. He simply said, **"You will learn and experience as you write."** So, I begin this book with that statement: **"Let's take this walk of faith together."** Initially, I had written, *"Your faith journey begins now,"* but our faith journey started a long time ago. What we sometimes lack is clarity and direction.

This one word, "Faith," will be my only focus for the year 2024, and hopefully, we will grasp this divine technology that we need to establish the kingdom of heaven on earth.

The instructions to me are very clear. Every breath I take, every blog post I write, every business transaction, all that I do in business, church, personal life, community, and studies will be a step of faith in 2024.

As I write this preface, my wife has been overseas working since October 2022. I see her only when I travel. I am running two businesses at home. We are drowning in credit card debt, paying both a mortgage and rent because we are constructing our home and have exhausted all our finances, and the house is still not complete. We had someone import a car because the one we are driving is really old. We have an application at the bank that has been pending for over eight weeks, and we have not heard anything positive or negative because of a bad debt we had over seven years ago that is being investigated. Apparently, we were victims of some apparent shady business practices of the debt collection agency that the bank used to recover their money. So when we thought we had cleared our loan, the collection agency had not paid the money over, and left a small balance that the bank wrote off.

The world is just recovering from the global pandemic known as COVID-19. The medical world is struggling; governments are not addressing the needs of the common people; crime is at an all-time high, and fatal accidents have risen to epic proportions. This I can speak to because we are dealing with a generation of drivers who grew up playing video games like “Need for Speed” and “Grand Theft Auto.” These young drivers actually drive on our roads as if they are immortal and have many lives to spare.

Where is faith in all this? What part does the church play in rectifying the ills in society? How effective have we been in repairing the breaches?

While we can look at the chaos in and around us, this book will not address the response of the masses or how the church needs to approach these issues. This book targets the one who can make a difference in their sphere of influence. In essence, you are the one. If my own journey and theological reflections can inspire and activate faith in you to believe God for the impossible and to also believe you have the capacity to make a difference, that is enough. I believe in the power of one. I believe in you.

Faith is not an easy walk, though it is a word that is thrown around loosely by believers. I hope we can unpack this word from every possible angle so that together we can learn to walk the walk and not just talk. It will be an interesting journey if you choose to take this with me.

There is one key verse that has sparked the need to have this conversation:

"I tell you that He will avenge them speedily. Nevertheless, when the Son of Man comes, will He really find faith on the earth?" (Luke 18:8 - NKJV).

Was this a prophetic utterance from our Master, or was He merely stating a concern? I will allow you the privilege to be the judge of that.

TABLE OF CONTENTS

INTRODUCTION

I will share many of my daily stories as I take this journey into the technology called faith. I was on my way from Kingston, Jamaica, after conducting some business. It was during the holiday season, so there was a lot of traffic on the road. I really wanted to take the highway that would bypass most of the traffic, but it required payment. When I checked how much money I had, I was short by a few cents—not dollars, just cents, an amount I normally pass by on the road.

I faced several choices. I could travel the old route and deal with the traffic since I didn't have the exact money for the toll. Or I could take the toll road and beg for a pardon, explaining that I was short by only a few pennies. Depending on who I encountered, I might receive a free pass, but I could also come across someone having a bad day, and that would not end well for me.

The third option, I believe, came from the voice of faith: **Just take the toll road and believe that by the time you reach the toll booth, the money will be there—nothing short.** As I sat in traffic, mulling over these options, I knew I was on a path of faith that required me to believe and act on what I believed. The problem was, I had no prior experience with this kind of money miracle, so it made me very nervous to take that route. Guess what choice I made: I decided to go the old route and deal with the traffic.

As we explore this topic of faith, we will learn that it is not an easy walk. We face these decisions every day, and in these small moments, God tests our faith to build our faith muscle. However, we often fail to act because, in reality, we don't believe that it will happen according to our faith. We expect and anticipate disappointment because that has been our experience.

CHAPTER 1

BEGINNINGS OF BEGINNINGS

The beginning is always a good place to start, so let's take some time to lay a foundation. On this topic of faith, there is much to cover, but every great construction needs a proper foundation. We are here because there was a creation, unless you believe in the idea of evolution, vis-à-vis, complex life emerging from absolutely nothing. It is not really far from the truth, but something is missing, or more so, Someone is missing.

I am fascinated by the doctrine of creation for two reasons: first, it introduces God, who has always existed, and second, it highlights His capacity to create worlds out of nothing. My interest in the doctrine of creation deepened after spending hours listening to Rabbis teach on the Torah. One particularly intriguing topic discussed by a professor is the concept of "Day," a key element of the creation story, as God created the world in "six days." How do we characterize the days of creation? We know there were six days, but how were these days measured? It wasn't until the fourth day that

God created the entities we use today to measure time (see Genesis 1:14-19).

What constituted a day before we were able to determine that a day has 24 hours? Was our capacity to measure time also affected by the fall? Wouldn't the way a "day" is measured change after the fall? Erickson presents six theories in his book "Christian Theology." My personal belief aligns with theory #4 – The Age-Day Theory. Erickson writes, *"The age-day theory is based upon the fact that the Hebrew word 'yom,' while it most frequently means a twenty-four-hour period, is not limited to that meaning. It can also mean epochs or long periods of time, and that is how it should be understood in this context. This view holds that God created in a series of acts over long periods of time. The geological and fossil records correspond to the days of his creative acts"* (Erickson, pg. 351).

When contemplating God, one must consider that He is eternal and has always existed. This concept is incomprehensible to the human mind, which perceives reality as having a beginning and an end. For a Supreme Being to have no beginning or end is beyond our understanding. Considering creation from the perspective of "days," we must recognize the infinite nature of the Creator, who is not limited by time, space, or matter. The second consideration is that the fall affected all of creation. Therefore, our way of measuring time and the nature of creation may have devolved because of the fall. What we know for sure is that there was a creation (hence a Creator) and a fall. Because humanity fell, salvation became necessary. Understanding the purpose of creation helps us decipher the intent of redemption, as restoration is promised after man's fall.

I listened to one of my professors as he discussed the purpose of creation; he referenced Psalms 19 and 104, which state that God created to **"show His greatness"** or to **"show His glory."** Another way to phrase this is to say God created to **"share"** His greatness and glory. I agree with Dr. Fairburn in his book "Life With the Trinity": *"In some ways, the Fall is the most difficult part of the Christian message, not because it is hard to understand but because its implications are hard to accept"* (Fairburn, pg. 84). How did the fall happen? God instructed the first man and woman that they could eat from any tree except one. A serpent beguiled Eve, leading her to disobey God. Interestingly, Adam did not converse with either his wife or the serpent; he acted on what was presented to him. James expounds on the process of the fall:

"Let no one say when he is tempted, 'I am being tempted by God,' for God cannot be tempted with evil, and he himself tempts no one. But each person is tempted when he is lured and enticed by his own desire. Then desire when it has conceived gives birth to sin, and sin when it is fully grown brings forth death." (James 1:13-15 - ESV).

Believers must be careful not to fall into the same trap. We cannot discuss creation without addressing the reality of the fall. These are two distinct highlights of Scripture embedded in the first three books of the Bible, summarizing what God created and what went wrong. Salvation became necessary because there was a fall, and there was a fall because there was a creation. Understanding man's fall helps us understand the need for a plan of redemption and, more so, the need for faith. But why would God want to redeem us? David asked a similar question and provided a glimpse of an answer:

"What is man that You are mindful of him, and the son of man that You visit him? For You have made him a little lower than the angels, and You have crowned him with glory and honor. You have made him to have dominion over the works of Your hands; You have put all things under his feet, all sheep and oxen—even the beasts of the field, the birds of the air, and the fish of the sea that pass through the paths of the seas." (Psalm 8:4-8 - NKJV).

If God had written off humanity as a failed experiment, wouldn't He also have to destroy all creation over which man was given dominion? Moreover, if man was created as God's image-bearer, wouldn't the destruction of man imply the destruction of some aspect of God Himself? These questions lead me to conclude that humanity is more intertwined with God than we realize. His choice to extend redemption to us highlights our value from a divine perspective. While man may think little of himself due to his shortcomings, God sees an eternal treasure worth saving.

In Genesis 1:1-25, we see God speaking existence into being. In six days, He created everything we know in the physical realm. It appears God did not create the world for Himself because, in Genesis 1:26, He made man in His image and likeness. Essentially, man is God's image-bearer and the crown jewel of His creative endeavors.

Regarding the distinction between image and likeness, I accept the view that "image" is created, but "likeness" is achieved through relationship. While man was created in a particular way, there was much room for relational interaction, as evidenced by God coming down in the cool of the day to fellowship with man. Why else would God come down to man? Another consideration is whether man, before losing divine favor, was able to go where God is. If not to build a relationship, why else would God come down in the cool of the day to fellowship with man? If likeness was a future goal, what role did the Tree of the Knowledge of Good and Evil play in the garden? Did God place it there to tempt or test man, or was it intended for a future reality? If man was immortal, why did he need to feed on the Tree of Life to maintain that reality?

I believe that while the image of God has been restored to the believer, likeness can only be achieved through a relationship. There is a principle in marriage that suggests a husband and wife begin to look alike after years of being together. Similarly, there is a measure of likeness achieved through face-to-face interaction. We see this with Jesus and His disciples. Scripture says the disciples were perceived to have been with Christ. After three years of walking with Jesus, it would have been hard to tell them apart. If this was true then, isn't it even more true for us today?

McGrath writes, *"The Christian tradition, basing itself largely upon the accounts of creation found in the book of Genesis, has insisted that humanity is the height of God's creation, set over and above the animal kingdom"* (McGrath, pg. 345). Man was created with the capacity to choose, a gift that proved detrimental to the entire human race. The concept of "free will" has been a point of controversy. Even today, theologians disagree about human beings having absolute free will, as it seems to diminish God's sovereignty. *"For Augustine, the total sovereignty of God and genuine human responsibility and freedom must be upheld at one and the same time"* (McGrath, pg. 351). Augustine believed in the sovereignty of God but denied human freedom. Pelagius upheld human free will but denied the sovereignty of God. McGrath posits that the term *"free will"* was not biblical but introduced into Western Christianity by Tertullian, a second-century theologian. Regardless of our position on free will, scripture shows that man chose to disobey God's direct command, plunging all humanity into sin.

We don't fully know what Adam was like before the fall. We know ourselves in the context of the fall, with all its limitations, but what was man like before the fall? We caught glimpses of extraordinary realities with Enoch, Moses, Abraham, Elijah, etc., but it wasn't until Christ that we saw man as he may have been before the fall. Jesus, as fully man (though fully God), demonstrated what man could be like before the fall.

A flawed aspect of doctrine was the belief that we cannot be like Christ, so His example was not something to strive for. Philippians 2 suggests He laid aside His divinity, walking the earth in full human capacity, setting a precedent for us. Jesus often alluded to the fact that His disciples (and by extension, us) could do what He did. In fact, we will do greater things. Why would the Teacher want His students to do greater things than Him? He also frequently referred to Himself as the **"Son of Man"** (see Matthew 8:20, Matthew 9:6, Matthew 11:19, Mark 8:31, Luke 9:26). Should members of the body of Christ accept doing less than what Christ did as a man?

The concept of being "Made in God's Image" is intriguing and a conversation I have been having for years now. A professor once said, **"God rules creation from without; man was created to rule from within."** This makes sense when considering how the world operates today. I often wonder why God doesn't intervene when man acts contrary to His nature. We see mass shootings, the desecration of the innocent, and other atrocities carried out by men with seemingly no divine intervention. As David laments, many people also cry out, **"Where is God?"** I believe the more fitting question is, **"Where is man?"** God asked that question of Adam, and He also asked it of Job:

"Now prepare yourself like a man; I will question you, and you shall answer Me. 'Where were you when I laid the foundations of the earth? Tell Me, if you have understanding. Who determined its measurements? Surely you know!'" (Job 38:3-5 - NKJV).

It is interesting that **"Surely you know!"** was not a question. Could it be that we have not learned our true role within the fabric of creation? Could it be that we struggle to grasp the reality of what has been restored after the fall by the coming of Jesus Christ into the world? I believe the original mandate given to man has not changed. One of the reasons for the coming of the Messiah is the restoration of the original intent, which includes:

- ∂ Being fruitful and multiplying.
- ∂ Filling the earth and subduing it.
- ∂ Replenishing the earth.
- ∂ Obeying God.

How does all this relate to the idea of faith? If this world is going to change, then our faith must be—and I will borrow a famous AI word—unwavering. Faith, defined in its simplest terms, is believing in God, and this is the quintessential struggle of every believer, whether we admit it or not, because God asks us to believe in realities that are out of this world. How does someone suffering from the debilitating symptoms of a cancer diagnosis believe they are already healed? How can someone drowning in debt believe they lack nothing? That all things are theirs? Yet, this is the call on the believer's life: to have faith. We have not only fallen from grace, but we have fallen from faith.

"All things were made by him; and without him was not any thing made that was made." (John 1:3 – NKJV).

I believe creation exists within God. In a sense—as my mentor teaches—He created a space within Himself for all that He created, and it is all held together by the Word of God. **"For in Him we live, move, and have our being" (Acts 17:28).** I believe humanity fell short of the glory of God through disobedience, causing the fall of humanity that reverberated throughout all creation. This is why creation groans for the manifestation of the sons of God (see Romans 8). I believe Jesus, God made flesh, came to restore humanity to its original state, which is both a present and future reality for the believer. This reality can only be accessed by an act of our will; fitting considering that it was an act of will that caused the fall.

My key idea as a theologian is that **"Faith Without Works is Dead."** We are called to give substance and evidence through faith to concepts and ideas for which we may have no initial proof. In a world of philosophy and intellectual ideas that formulate theories to deny God, faith comes at a cost. Even God's faith in humanity provoked Him to act, providing a means for our redemption. How much more should our faith in Him provoke us to believe in the One He sent out of love for humanity, despite knowing that many will reject Him? Faith should produce works despite any perceived outcomes.

As a writer, I am excited about God because there is no end to divine revelation about who He is. I hold certain doctrines loosely, allowing God to reveal Himself however He chooses. I know He will not contradict His Word, so my journey of faith continues into the depths of God.

Consider these two implications of the doctrine of creation:

1. Everything that exists has value because, while it is not God, it has been made by Him. He made it because He was pleased to do so, and it was good in His sight. Each part has its place, as God intended. God loves all His creation, not just certain parts of it. Thus, we should also have concern for all of it, preserving, guarding, and developing what God has made. We are part of the creation, but only a part. While God intended us to use the creation for our own needs, we are also to have dominion over it, governing it for its good. Therefore, we have a large stake in ecological concerns. Christians should be at the forefront of concern for the preservation and welfare of creation because it is God's handiwork (Erickson, pg. 356).

2. Nothing other than God is self-sufficient or eternal. Everything else, every object and being, derives its existence from Him and exists to do His will. Only God deserves our worship. Everything else exists for His sake, not He for its sake. Although we highly respect creation, since it has been made by Him, we must maintain a clear distinction between God and it.

Through redemption, believers in Jesus Christ cannot continue to use the fall to absolve themselves of responsibility toward God's created world. We have always had a role, both post- and pre-fall. Our "works" derived from our "faith" provide substance and establish evidence of the unseen world and the movements and interactions of our Father, who is Spirit, in the lives of His prized creation.

CHAPTER 2

JUST BELIEVE

"What do you mean, 'If I can'?" Jesus asked. "Anything is possible if a person believes." (Mark 9:23 - NLT).

When Jesus walked the earth, I imagine it was much easier for people to believe in Him because they could see His reputation, witness His actions, hear His words, and He was within reach. They could touch Him, see Him, smell Him, and hear Him. Jesus reiterated to many who came to Him that their **"faith made them well,"** suggesting that one simply needed to believe for their desired need to manifest.

So, what happened? If we are simply asked to **"Just believe,"** why does it seem so hard to produce miracles?

Being called upon to have faith is no walk in the park. Faith will cost you everything, and I am of the opinion that the price is too high for many.

As I write this chapter, I have been a little obsessed with my blood pressure. A few years ago, I was diagnosed with hypertension and was put on medication. I have never liked the idea of drugs because I believe they do damage over time. Drugs address symptoms but not the root of the disease, so essentially, they are a form of damage control, not a cure in and of themselves. My father took drugs all his life, and the latter part of his life was a horrible experience for us as his family because he literally lost his mind. I believe a human being should have a sharp mind to the very end. There is no reason for us to develop Alzheimer's and other mental diseases as we age, so something is to be blamed for that. Age comes with wisdom, not a loss of it.

In any case, long-term use of drugs is not on my bucket list. My intention was always to get off the drugs, so I changed my diet, joined a gym, and started doing what was necessary. My blood pressure actually went lower than it should be normally. So, my good doctor reduced my medication but would not take me completely off it.

I remember years ago, God had asked me a question, **"At what point will you believe?"** At the time, I was on a barrage of drugs for all kinds of ailments. I threw away the pills but went back to the doctor a few weeks later when the symptoms were just overbearing. Here I was again, faced with the same predicament.

I have had the blood pressure medication put aside for any apparent emergency. Being sensitive (what they call anxiety) doesn't help much, especially being home alone as my wife works and travels. It is always a trying period where I come face to face with my own mortality and fear. I have been trying out a new diet that didn't seem to help my blood pressure much. Additionally, I have taken a more natural approach, using nature's ingredients instead of drugs made up of ingredients I cannot pronounce. I am sure some reading this can relate.

My blood pressure just refuses to normalize, so I am fighting the urge to go back on the drugs. I actually took one of the pills, and I didn't feel good at all. Taking drugs can sometimes be worse than the symptoms of any sickness, real or perceived.

So, here I am, writing my memoir and penning a chapter titled **"Just Believe."** So, let's explore this in the very midst of my apparent turmoil. The use of the word "Just" means leaving no room for anything else. No doubts, no what-ifs, without questioning—it is a solid stance that you will believe for something that is not yet a manifested reality. In this case, it means believing that my blood pressure will normalize without any interference from drugs or that what is happening in my body is normal and no damage will occur (which I'm sure is a possibility). This is harder than it sounds.

"Just believe" means acknowledging our mortality and the fact that our decision to act only on faith and nothing else could prove detrimental if it fails to produce an alternate reality to the one we are presently facing. It is a surrender of all, including our very life and our fear of dying alone, not getting any help on time, being unable to even call for help, and just the sheer helplessness of any reality that fear conjures up in our imagination. It is a real battle indeed, but as a believer, what is our recourse when faced with a real issue?

It is one thing to try and advise others who are going through a "struggle" to just believe, but when we are the ones called upon to exercise our own advice, that is when the rubber hits the road. I have to make a decision at the risk of everything. It may mean that this book never gets published; it may mean I don't live to see my children or grandchildren; it may mean losing it all. But we cannot preach and teach "faith" and not practice what we teach. In moments of weakness, I tend to go back to what is familiar or what is recommended by mainstream media, but I know it is not a fixed solution. The goal is always to get to that place where I am walking in absolute faith.

"Just believe" is the immediate call, and I don't advise anyone to make such a leap as to get off all medical drugs unless you have made up your mind to lose everything. I am still not perfect where this is concerned, but I am working on it.

"For whoever desires to save his life will lose it, but whoever loses his life for My sake and the gospel's will save it." (Mark 8:35 - NKJV).

You may be going through one of the hardest seasons of your life. I can tell you from experience that God gauges just how much you go through, and it is NEVER more than you can bear. He knows your limits and considers even your mindset when it comes to what you experience, so you can trust that whatever you are going through, somehow, you are strong enough. Be encouraged, and seek to find the courage to **"Just believe."**

I read in a book recently a very interesting thought, **"If you cannot overcome fear, then do it afraid."** I know what it is like to be afraid, no, to be terrified. I have had those nights when I was afraid to fall asleep because I thought that was it; if I fell asleep, I would not wake up. I know what it is like, but often, our experiences are allowed because they are part of the process. One of the hardest lessons God will ever have to teach one of His children is to **"Have faith."** You can do it. We can do it.

"But may the God of all grace, who called us to His eternal glory by Christ Jesus, after you have suffered a while, perfect, establish, strengthen, and settle you." (1 Peter 5:10 - NKJV).

You will walk away from this with a powerful testimony if you **"Just believe."** Rest assured, if you are reading this, then faith is as potent as it has ever been, and your **"faith has made you well."**

CHAPTER 3

MOUNTAIN-MOVING FAITH

At the foot of the mountain, a large crowd was waiting for them. A man came and knelt before Jesus and said, "Lord, have mercy on my son. He has seizures and suffers terribly. He often falls into the fire or into the water. So I brought him to your disciples, but they couldn't heal him." Jesus said, "You faithless and corrupt people! How long must I be with you? How long must I put up with you? Bring the boy here to me." Then Jesus rebuked the demon in the boy, and it left him. From that moment the boy was well. Afterward, the disciples asked Jesus privately, "Why couldn't we cast out that demon?" "You don't have enough faith," Jesus told them. "I tell you the truth, if you had faith even as small as a mustard seed, you could say to this mountain, 'Move from here to there,' and it would move. Nothing would be impossible." (Matthew 17:14-21 - NLT).

It amazes me how, in the generation we now live in, Pentecostals will spend a whole night trying to cast out a "demon" and walk away thinking they have been successful instead of admitting their failure. I believe this is the contrast between those who have a relationship with the Lord and those who do not. The disciples went to Jesus and asked, **"Why couldn't we cast out that demon?"** Many would ask today, **"Why couldn't we heal that blind man?" "Why couldn't we heal that person who died from cancer?" "Why couldn't we raise that kid from the dead?"** If we dared to ask, I believe the answer would still be the same: **"You don't have enough faith."** The bigger question is, **"What is smaller than a mustard seed?"** Is our faith really that minute that it cannot reproduce the realities of heaven here on earth?

My supernatural journey started over a decade ago with very few verifiable miracles. I have prayed for a cancer patient who died the very next day. I have seen my neighbor die from asphyxiation, leaving her young children behind, and I couldn't change it. My faith hardly produces tangible results, and yet I still pursue that reality. A pastor once asked me, **"Why do you believe in raising the dead? You've never seen it happen."** I believe because the Bible says I can.

"And as you go, preach, saying, 'The kingdom of heaven is at hand.' Heal the sick, cleanse the lepers, raise the dead, cast out demons. Freely you have received, freely give." (Matthew 10:7-8 - NKJV).

I don't believe for a second that the mandate of the church has changed. I don't believe we have less power than the early church. I do believe we are missing some key spiritual practices, and I do believe we have regressed and allowed Christianity to become something it was not meant to be. For the most part, the church today looks like the church in Jesus' day with Pharisees, Scribes, and Teachers of the Law who are incapable of seeing Jesus standing before them because their theology dictates who God is, how God operates, and how God should show Himself. Our expectations of what we perceive God to be can cause us to miss our day of visitation.

Faith makes all things possible. The lack of faith makes room for the reality of the impossible to overcome us. It is the lack of faith that gave birth to the idea of **"That is impossible."**

Adam and Eve were created in a limitless expanse of creation—an ever-expanding reality where nothing (absolutely nothing) was impossible. The only purpose faith served in their lives was to obey God in regards to what they had no knowledge about. They didn't need faith to carry out their rule and dominion in the created space; they just knew they could. The very idea of **"I can't do that"** never existed for them until the fall. They never knew fear until the fall.

One of Jesus' central messages in re-educating humanity about who they were created to be is a matter of faith. His statements may seem far-fetched because of our inexperience in seeing manifestations of another world superimposing on ours, but it doesn't make them any less true. Jesus says that if we believe, we can say to a mountain **"Be thou removed"** and it will be done for us. I have heard myriads of interpretations about this text, mostly leaning towards a metaphoric interpretation. The general consensus seems to be that Jesus was not speaking about a physical mountain, but any circumstance or situation that may be standing in our path. We may even demonize the mountain, but what if this was a literal statement?

Let us consider the life of the one who made this statement. He turned water to wine, gave sight to the blind, hearing to the deaf, speech to the mute, and strength to the legs of the lame. He raised people from the dead, including Lazarus, who was dead for four days. Consider this: the Jews believe that the soul of a person stays around for three days after they die before departing this realm. Consider also that science proves that the body enters a stage of decomposition on the third day. They didn't have access to what we have access to today, where the blood of a person is removed and replaced with a certain liquid that slows the decomposition process, especially in our day when we take weeks or months to bury someone. We also see Jesus walking on water, calming a raging storm by speaking to it, and feeding multitudes of people with a box lunch. Everything listed here is considered **"impossible"** in our time, but Jesus says it is not. The question then arises, why are we not seeing these things happen as naturally as we breathe?

Telling a believer they don't have enough faith is seen as an insult. We would prefer to formulate perceived results that cannot be verified instead of doing what the disciples did. They went to Jesus and asked, **"Why couldn't we do it?"** We should be asking this same question and seeking an answer from the Master. We know nothing has changed. God has not changed His mind. There are many promises in Scripture that we often fail to see manifest in our own lives, and no matter how indoctrinated we become to explain our ineffectiveness and seeming powerlessness, it always comes back to the same response: **"You don't have enough faith."**

There are aspects of our fundamental make-up that we tend to avoid or disown because we choose not to face up to certain realities. For me, I probe my mind to seek the source of my problems. Faith is something I have contemplated well and hard, and I do not find a lack of faith within myself, yet my results are minute. What I do find within myself is the presence of doubt, fear, and unbelief. Some would say faith and unbelief cannot coexist in the same vessel. I disagree:

"Immediately the father of the child cried out and said with tears, 'Lord, I believe; help my unbelief!'" (Mark 9:24 - NKJV).

There are things we don't want to be true, so we either ignore their reality or deny their existence, but that doesn't erase their effect because they are present. Honesty and transparency are lacking in the body of Christ, especially among us as leaders, who think the expectations placed on us are so forbearing that we cannot admit to weaknesses and failures. This often leads to us struggling in isolation or in secret, thus living double and triple lives. We may be one—body, soul, and spirit—but we can be as fragmented as the idea of existing in multi-dimensional realms. For example, and this goes way beyond my understanding, one can be a Christian leader, even a pastor, and a homosexual simultaneously. A lack of honesty can cause us to live fragmented lives, and I believe one of the goals of being a believer is to become **"whole"** or **"one"** with ourselves. Union with God is not possible for the one who is fragmented.

"And he said unto him, Arise, go thy way: thy faith hath made thee whole." (Luke 17:19 - KJV).

We need faith in order to de-fragment. If we use **"mountain"** as a metaphor, then fragmentation is one of those huge mountains we need to move in order to come into the reality of who we are in God, and to fully understand and walk in our **"mountain-moving"** authority.

CHAPTER 4

THE POWER OF THE WORD

The Doctrine of Scripture is foundational to Christian theology because it deals with the authority and interpretation of the Bible as the inspired Word of God. As Author Millard J. Erickson posits, *"The general revelation of God has been found in three areas: nature, history, and humanity"* (Christian Theology, pg. 121). Scripture falls into the area of history as it documents God's interaction with humanity from creation to a time prophesied but not yet. There are two words that are key in examining this doctrine: inerrancy and infallibility.

The term "inerrancy" has been debatable for some time. It is defined as a claim to the truthfulness and authority of Scripture by virtue of God being the author. If the Bible is from God, then the Bible is true, without errors, and authoritative. It means, as a believer, we can trust the text, even when we have no grid for what is written or an understanding of certain texts of Scripture. What may seem like contradictions are really our limited perception of both the written word and the experience of the human writer. As one of my professors said, when we say the Bible is inerrant, we are making a statement about God, so we can affirm the truthfulness of Scripture because God is the Author.

In my church denomination, our creed is that the Bible is our rule of faith. Our doctrine reads: *"We believe that the Bible—both Old and New Testaments—is the inspired Word of God. The Bible is God's revelation of Himself and His will to humankind, sufficient for instruction in salvation and daily Christian living. The Bible is the Christian's rule of faith and practice."* We do affirm that the Bible is without error and that any misconceptions come about from our limited experience and purview. As long as the focus is on us and our interpretation of Scripture, we create the possibility of walking in error, but affirming, as my professor said, the inerrancy of Scripture, it keeps our focus on God, thereby keeping us open to how He chooses to reveal Himself to the seeker through the written text.

To say that the Scriptures are infallible means that they are incapable of leading believers astray in matters of faith and practice. The concept of infallibility affirms that the teachings and truths found in the Bible are trustworthy, reliable, and free from error when it comes to guiding individuals in matters of salvation, faith, and Christian living.

Infallibility is closely related to the concept of inerrancy, which asserts that the original manuscripts of the Bible are without error. While inerrancy focuses on the absence of mistakes or contradictions in the text, infallibility emphasizes the trustworthiness and reliability of the teachings and doctrines presented in the Scriptures.

I once had an interesting debate with a pastor about a particular text. I interpreted the text literally, to which he responded, *"That's not what the text is saying."* He proceeded to give an interpretation that, to me, changed the meaning of what was written. I was accused of being my own authority when it came to Scripture, even though I held an interpretation that was literally what was written. So, the question then arises, in relation to the doctrine of Scripture, who is the authority behind its interpretation? Can we put confidence in the voice in our head? Our own intuition or understanding? The safest path to take is to allow Scripture to be the authority on itself. McGrath writes, *"...Christian theology was ultimately grounded in Scripture...reformers such as Luther and Calvin argued for the need to return to Scripture as the primary and critical source of Christian theology. The slogan "by Scripture alone" (sola scriptura) became characteristic of the Protestant reformers, expressing their belief that Scripture was the sole necessary and sufficient source of Christian theology."* (Christian Theology, pg. 59). While, for the most part, most denominations have settled on what is labeled **"sound doctrine,"** I believe the correct approach in each age and as knowledge increases is to go back to Scripture and revisit **"all doctrines."**

Let's take, for example, the account of Joshua. Joshua told the sun and moon to stand still (see Joshua 10:12-13), which they did. Joshua may not have known that it was the earth orbiting the sun, but science has now made this common knowledge. For the sun to stand still, the entire solar system had to stop moving for the duration of that time, which would have thrown out the very laws that govern times and seasons. Could this be the reason why we have a leap year? There are many doctrines that came about through intellectual debates that may need to be revisited now that we know a little bit more.

The main text that sums up what Scripture says about itself is 2 Timothy 3:16, **"All scripture is given by inspiration of God, and is profitable for doctrine, for reproof, for correction, for instruction in righteousness."** The text of scripture was not written to **"our standard of accuracy,"** which means due consideration must be given to that fact in any attempt to achieve some measure of interpretation of any particular text.

Scripture is a revelation (revealing of), but is not the only form of special revelation. It is a historical record of several different forms of special revelation. Four are primarily discussed: God acting directly, God speaking through messengers, God entering history directly and personally through the incarnation and, the last, God giving us a written record as a summary of the first three, which emphasizes the place and importance of Scripture. It is difficult then to dispute the inerrancy and infallibility of scripture, according to Author Millard J. Erickson, because God is the author.

The language used in Scripture is authoritative, and as Paul writes, **"profitable for doctrine, reproof, correction and instruction in righteousness,"** which are the summative levels of the Christian's journey back to God. History, as recorded by Scripture, is a path already designed for the believer to walk. Erickson writes, *"...history is the laboratory in which theology tests its ideas, (so) we must conclude that the departure from belief in the complete trustworthiness of the Bible is a very serious step....in terms of what happens to other doctrines as a result"* (Christian Theology, pg. 196).

As a student of both conservative and mystical theology—of theology that targets the head and that which targets the heart—I wholeheartedly believe in the inerrancy and infallibility of Scripture, but I will argue on many related topics that are often labeled **"sound doctrine."** Paul had experiences I can only fantasize about, yet he said, **"That I might know Him…" (see Philippians 3:10).** He further declared, **"For I determined not to know any thing among you, save Jesus Christ, and him crucified" (1 Corinthians 2:2 – KJV).** There are certain rules that govern the foundation of any building that, if tampered with, can result in catastrophe when a building is put on it. The foundation must be fixed and adhere to all governing rules for the building to stand. But the buildings will be different, serving different purposes. So it is with us who are the temple of

God. The foundation has been set... **"we know nothing, except Christ crucified,"** but each temple will be built differently to serve different purposes.

I have adopted the key idea **"Faith Without Works is Dead,"** which pretty much sums up my Christian journey in the last decade or so and is a theme that will be repeated throughout this book. The Key Idea **"Faith Without Works is Dead"** is adapted from the idea presented by Apostle James writings where he states in writing to the twelve tribes of Israel: **"But do you want to know, O foolish man, that faith without works is dead? Was not Abraham our father justified by works when he offered Isaac his son on the altar? Do you see that faith was working together with his works, and by works faith was made perfect?" (James 2:20-23).**

Faith requires us to do something and is not sufficient in and of itself. We believe to be saved, but to produce the works, we must act on our faith. **Jesus answered and said unto them, This is the work of God, that ye believe on him whom he hath sent (John 6:29 - KJV).** Paul goes further to say: **"For the kingdom of God is not in word, but in power" (1 Corinthians 4:20 - KJV).** And additionally, **"And my speech and my preaching was not with enticing words of man's wisdom, but in demonstration of the Spirit and of power: That your faith should not stand in the wisdom of men, but in the power of God" (1 Corinthians 2:4-5 - KJV).** The walk of faith is also the work of faith. It is a believer's capacity to bring the realities of heaven to earth, and Scripture is our sole authority in both understanding and executing this task through the indwelling of the Spirit of God.

In the beginning, we see the Spirit of God hovering over what was called **"void and darkness."** Another word used is **"chaos."** God spoke (the Word of God who was from the beginning), and the Spirit manifested what was spoken. Similarly, the Holy Spirit in our lives quickens in order to bring the **"Word of God"** spoken into reality. Thus, salvation is achieved by confession and faith (see Romans 10:9), and this same measure of faith can also lead to deliverance, healing, miracles, signs, wonders, and all things supernatural (see Mark 16:16-20).

We can receive salvation and never save a soul, heal a sick person, cast out a demon, or raise anyone from the dead, but still receive the benefits of salvation because it is rooted and grounded in what was accomplished by Jesus Christ and on nothing that we do. But it doesn't mean that potentially we cannot and should not do all that was listed above. Personally, if I am going to believe in the infallibility and inerrancy of Scripture, then I must also believe that the same experiences the writers of the text had are also available to me. I love the way James says it:

Elias was a man subject to like passions as we are, and he prayed earnestly that it might not rain: and it rained not on the earth by the space of three years and six months. (James 5:17 - KJV).

What message was James trying to convey? This is the foundation for my own ministry as an author as I continue to seek the heart of God. I must not only believe that God is, but I must also believe that He is a rewarder to those who diligently seek Him (see Hebrews 11:6). One of the key words in that text is **"rewarder."** The original word used is **"misthapodotés,"** which speaks to one who pays wages. The benefits of our faith in God yield tangible returns. It is not to say we go to God for what we can get, but understanding that in having God, we lack nothing.

Author Millard J. Erickson sums this up nicely: *"In a world in which there are so many erroneous conceptions and so many opinions, the Bible is a sure source of guidance. For when correctly interpreted, it can be fully relied on in all that it teaches. It is a sure dependable, and trust-worthy authority."*

The Word of God is the basis for our faith. It is God's spoken Word in written form. Jesus is God's Living Word. What is spoken by Jesus and written in Scripture becomes our authority in faith. We can have what is written because God already said it, and it is His Word that frames our true reality. God said you are healed. He said you are blessed; you lack nothing. You are more than a conqueror. He said your faith can produce a completely different reality than what you may be facing at this moment. Where it seems like God is absent, by an extension of our faith, God becomes present. He is as close to us as the air we breathe, never too far away, and we access Him by faith.

Read the Word and take notes. If God already said it, it is already yours. It is already done.

CHAPTER 5

BACK TO THE BEGINNING

Faith is not needed where there is no man. So, in the beginning, before man was created, there was no need for faith. It didn't exist in any context. The moment Adam and Eve were created, faith came into existence. Faith is the connecting principle between the visible and the invisible realm. It is the technology by which the visible is able to see with absolute clarity that which is not visible. Faith makes it possible for humans to connect with the divine.

One of the issues that affects our capacity to see and relate to the unseen world has to do with our understanding of frequency. If you are from a traditional church like myself, you may not have heard this word in relation to spirituality. Everything vibrates at a certain frequency. If you are a fan of movies, there is one called Lucy that has some very interesting concepts. In one scene, she describes time by using a moving car as an example. She says if the car moves fast enough, it will not be seen with the human eye. We could also use a fly, for example. From its perspective, we are moving in slow motion. From our perspective, we wonder how a fly can move so fast, and if they are flying fast enough, you may not be able to catch them with your physical eyes.

The unseen realm is also bound by the laws of frequency. Angels, for example, vibrate at such a high frequency that they are not easily seen unless they take on a form that vibrates at a lower frequency. The only thing that allows us to see what is not there is faith.

"Now faith is the substance of things hoped for, the evidence of things not seen." (Hebrews 11:1 - NKJV).

Let's look at this verse in another translation:

"The fundamental fact of existence is that this trust in God, this faith, is the firm foundation under everything that makes life worth living. It's our handle on what we can't see. The act of faith is what distinguished our ancestors, set them above the crowd." (Hebrews 11:1-2 - MSG).

Have you ever heard God ask you, ***"Do you trust Me?"***

The Bible shows us a world where anything is possible. Our reality shows us a world of self-sufficiency, where **"impossible"** has become a staple word on the lips of many, even in the community of **"faith." "I can't"** is spoken in almost every context, even though the Biblical narrative says, **"I can."**

Underachievement is the order of the day. The poor are having many children they cannot adequately care for, while the rich are having only a few children. Our school system dumps hundreds, if not thousands, of illiterate, underachieved children into society every year who take minimum wage jobs and are tempted with the possibility of earning through **"unjust"** means or not at all. What is lacking is not just opportunities for better but the empowerment needed to re-condition a youth's mind that they can choose to become great without breaking the law. What is lacking is a belief in their own self-actualization. Every single human being has the capacity to **"become,"** and we choose what to become, and faith is the mode of transportation.

Faith, by its very nature, extends beyond the physical and connects with the spiritual realm. It is the bridge that connects our present reality with the limitless possibilities of God's mind and heart for creation. It was His idea to create man, and man was created with the capacity to do certain things that was affected by the fall. When we say **"I can,"** we are not merely expressing a personal belief but aligning ourselves with the divine potential within us. This potential is often stifled by societal norms, personal insecurities, and the pervasive doubt that permeates our world.

Consider the story of Abraham, who was promised descendants as numerous as the stars despite his old age and Sarah's barrenness. It was his faith that made him righteous in God's eyes and enabled him to see beyond the physical limitations of his circumstances. Abraham's journey teaches us that faith is not about what we see but about trusting in what God has said, even when it seems impossible. Today, rationality and empirical evidence are highly valued, and faith can often be seen as outdated or irrelevant. But the essence of faith is timeless. It challenges us to look beyond the immediate and the tangible, urging us to trust in a higher power and a greater plan. Faith is what empowers us to envision a new world and all its possibilities, even when faced with overwhelming evidence to the contrary.

I have been dabbling in computers since the days when we needed to type **"win"** for Windows to open. Some will remember the black and white cow that appeared at the introduction of Windows. We have come a long way. But one thing I have learned with devices is that whenever they start to act up or give trouble, the first step in troubleshooting is to do a hard reset. In most cases, that usually fixes the problem. It means the device—be it a laptop, desktop, phone, or tablet—has picked up something that is affecting its original functionality. A reset sets it back to a previous point when it was working perfectly.

Christianity, influenced by indoctrination based on incorrect contexts and interpretations by those who saw the movement as a means of exploitation, has become something it was never meant to be. Instead of being an organic movement with the potential to transform the earth, it has become another religion with a focus on everything but a relational experience of the divine. This truncates the effectiveness of faith, turning it into a purely work-based, man-inspired movement divided into many denominations, with everyone wanting to be right and everyone else wrong. The truth is, maybe this was the only way Christianity would have survived all these centuries. Since the days of Jesus Christ, there has been great opposition from those who wish only to remove the idea of the Messiah from history. It is an absolute miracle that Christianity survived, and even today, there is great opposition directed against **"The Way."** Regardless, there is a need for a hard reset. We must journey back to the beginning when faith was at its most potent form and recalibrate. But first, we must be willing to admit that where we are and what we are doing is actually not working. It is not producing the results that faith was meant to produce, and because of that, the world is suffering greatly.

I have had the privilege of studying Christian history in my pursuit of a master's in theological studies. One thing is clear: in every epoch, there was always a remnant who would lay aside the common knowledge and beliefs and go back to Scripture with a fresh approach, unhindered by dogma or preconceived ideas. It is a place of **"no-thing"** where God is able to reveal **"some-thing new."** Going back to the starting point allows us to start afresh in gaining an understanding of what, for example, faith is and how it should operate in our lives. We can never be fully effective in our walk of faith when we are inundated with the baggage of a perceived reality that we wish to be true but is not. Let's look at an example.

"And He Himself gave some to be apostles, some prophets, some evangelists, and some pastors and teachers, for the equipping of the saints for the work of ministry, for the edifying of the body of Christ, till we all come to the unity of the faith and of the knowledge of the Son of God, to a perfect man, to the measure of the stature of the fullness of Christ; that we should no longer be children, tossed to and fro and carried about with every wind of doctrine, by the trickery of men, in the cunning craftiness of deceitful plotting, but, speaking the truth in love, may grow up in all things into Him who is the head—Christ—from whom the whole body, joined and knit together by what every joint supplies, according to the effective working by which every part does its share, causes growth of the body for the edifying of itself in love." (Ephesians 4:11-16 - NKJV).

There's a lot we could unpack from this, which would fill a whole volume by itself, but let's just focus on some key areas. There are many denominations that oppose the **"five-fold"** ministry, claiming it was for the early church but not for the modern church today. In my denomination, we give ministerial licenses to deacons and pastors, but we don't recognize the offices of evangelists, teachers, prophets, and apostles. In our context, anyone can teach who is willing to do so, but it is not a recognized office (gift). The problem with this approach is that we cannot experience the promises in this text unless all five of these gifts are operating in the church. The promises are:

∂ Equipping of the saints for the work of the ministry.

∂ Edifying of the body of Christ.

∂ Unity of the faith.

∂ Knowledge of the Son of God.

∂ A perfect man.

∂ The fullness of Christ.

∂ Maturing as a son of God.

∂ Perfect love.

∂ Growing up into the head—who is Christ.

We want the benefits without having to go through the process, and that is not how spiritual laws work. A hard reset back to the beginning would have a denomination or local church revisiting this text and re-examining their doctrine regarding what is written here, making the necessary adjustments to facilitate the functioning of these gifts (offices) in the local church. This is just one example of many, but you get the idea.

When we find ourselves struggling to actualize the promises of God in our lives, it means we have picked up a bug that is affecting us and preventing us from functioning from that original place and position that God created us to be. When this happens, we must go back to the beginning and start again. I have had to do this in my own life when God shifts me to a different level.

I grew up in a church that didn't emphasize the supernatural. I literally had no clue that God could heal someone from cancer or even raise the dead. When God pulled me into that arena, I felt like I was losing my mind. I had to reset because I realized that what I was learning was scriptural. It was always there—written, recorded, set in eternal stone—but how I read it and never saw it is a mystery to me. I have learned not to ignore what is written, no matter how far-fetched it seems.

The same thing happened when God pulled me even higher into what is called **"mystical theology."** This level cost me everything. My then-pastor actually told a friend of mine that *"I had great potential, but I went and made a mess of myself."* I lost friends, influence, and my voice—it was one of the greatest resets that I had experienced to date.

Going back to the beginning is not an **"Egypt-Exodus"** scenario where we want to return to what we are comfortable with. It is about going back to that original place where the thoughts of God are clear and pure before becoming tainted with our own perceptions and ideas, and starting from there. I understand now why Paul made certain statements like:

"Yet indeed I also count all things loss for the excellence of the knowledge of Christ Jesus my Lord, for whom I have suffered the loss of all things, and count them as rubbish, that I may gain Christ and be found in Him, not having my own righteousness, which is from the law, but that which is through faith in Christ, the righteousness which is from God by faith." (Philippians 3:8-9 - NKJV).

So many of us have immortalized what we know—or what we think we know—to our own detriment, but if we release what we know, we will make room for God to reveal what we do not yet know. One of the things that severely hampers our walk of faith is that we leave no room for God to reveal anything outside of what we already know.

"But as it is written: 'Eye has not seen, nor ear heard, nor have entered into the heart of man the things which God has prepared for those who love Him.'" (1 Corinthians 2:9 - NKJV).

Your smartphone can learn and adapt through consistent use, but eventually, it can pick up something that throws it completely off balance. Suddenly, it is not doing what it was created to do efficiently. Resetting it erases completely what it has learned and adapted to, allowing it to start again from its original point where it was most potent and its integrity intact. This reset is necessary for us as well, especially now when the groaning of creation is increasing for the manifestation of the sons of God. That is where I am heading, and that is the call I answered. Will you also answer the call?

CHAPTER 6

WE REAP WHAT WE SOW

"For as the body without the spirit is dead, so faith without works is dead also." (James 2:26 - NKJV).

Faith is not just our belief that produces good. The decisions we make and the actions we take today are seeds we sow for future cultivation. Sometimes, the harvest we yield is not a pleasant one. This is the danger of solely living in the moment without considering the future.

I got married and my father died in the same year, two months apart. We made some decisions then in order to have a good wedding and a good start to our marriage that may not have been completely sober financial decisions. So our marriage started in the red and went downhill for a while as it was also the season when I was trying to build my business as an entrepreneur. We fell into bad debt with the bank and our account was passed on to a debt collector. Miraculously—only God—we were able to settle that debt within a few short months, and it was behind us, or so we thought.

Nine years later, we have been driving an old car for many years and felt it was time to make a change. We made a bold move to ask someone to import the car that we wanted. Within a few weeks, the car was ready for purchase, so I went to the bank to apply for a car loan. This was when all our troubles started. When they ran our credit report, the language used was that our loan was not **"paid off"** but **"written off,"** suggesting that it was not paid. This turned into a weeks-long battle between us and the bank. They had no records of payments as they wiped their system every seven years. They couldn't even tell us who the collection agency they passed our account to was. It was by divine intervention, while sitting in the bank, that God told me to google a certain keyword, and I called the first company that came up, and they found my records. Sadly, they could not give me the proof I needed, so the battle intensified. I now had two applications with two separate creditors going back and forth, trying to convince them of a loan I paid off that was showing up as not paid off. The prospects of us getting the approval for the loan were slowly diminishing into a negative outcome, and we were both concerned and apprehensive. This went on for months.

I heard the voice of the Lord tell me to write a letter explaining my side of the story to give to the lending institutions along with all the other needed paperwork. I obeyed. All this was happening while we were in the latter and most expensive part of constructing our home, trying to get it finished because we were paying both mortgage and rent. It was a really trying time. I had a few nights where my sleep was very light as my mind kept thinking about the fact that as someone who values integrity, the financial system in my nation was trying to make me look like someone who didn't pay his debts.

The manager of the company who imported the car had to move his office, and after two months of having the car sitting on his car lot, he now had nowhere to store the car, so he took it to my home and parked it there. Now I had a car sitting on my porch that I wasn't sure how it would be paid for, but God.

One of the financial institutions came back with a negative response. They said I wasn't earning enough money. So it was now down to one bank, and we continued to wait. The new year started and was moving quickly. Somewhere close to the end of January, we were led to apply at a smaller bank, where we had no relationship or history whatsoever. My wife also had an uncle who operated a loan company, so we also approached him. In a short time (less than two weeks), we were approved for both loans. The other bank, who had our application for months, said they finally figured out how to get my loan approved after many back and forths, but I was able to tell them we were okay. We started the paperwork, and on February 21, 2024, I was driving our new car, and the old car was sold to my big brother. It got a little emotional to part with her, but she is still in the family.

Someone once said that faith untested is no faith at all. I believe God allows us to walk through varying circumstances, and it is not just about testing how strong our faith is but building our faith. Imagine how long it took Jesus to convince a few men who saw themselves as just fishermen and the like that they could walk on water. But the process of growing our faith doesn't start there. It begins with learning that mere water can be changed into something else when the need calls for it. We are taught also that by faith, a little can feed a multitude. The prosperity era of the gospel messed up our consciousness and set us back a bit in growing our faith. We failed to embrace the seasons designed to teach us faith, believing that faith should absolve any possibility of suffering and discomfort. The Bible does say God's promises are yes and amen, but to get there, we often have to endure many **"no's."**

By faith, I can see myself and my wife travelling the world. So, it was no surprise that I was given a 10-year visa to travel to the United States of America. This became a necessity when my wife started to work on travel. In order to protect both our purity, I started to travel as often as I was able to find cheap tickets to buy. We also had to find some very cheap and often uncomfortable accommodations to facilitate these visitations. It was a very wearisome time.

I remember on two occasions, in a two-year span, I decided to go to my mother-in-law and spend three months, so I could visit my wife a few times instead of going back and forth between Jamaica and the US. My wife also loved the fact that we were both in the same country, though many hundreds of miles apart. These were times I also got to experience driving 40 hours across the United States on two separate occasions. On the first occasion, my wife was inheriting a car her cousin, who had studied for two years in the US, was leaving behind. Someone needed to take the car to her, and I volunteered. I had never done anything like that before, but I still took on the challenge. The morning I woke up, I realized there was a small engine oil leak beneath the car, and I didn't allow that to dissuade me. For the entire journey, my expectation was not faith but the fear that I would be stranded in the middle of nowhere, far from anyone I knew. It was a mind-boggling and fearful experience, but by then, I had learned to "do it afraid." This is necessary when building faith.

Those two three-month-long occasions became a seed planted that would produce a very uncomfortable experience in the future. While travelling on one occasion during our birth month (me and my wife celebrate our birthdays in November), I was taken to the "room" where my phone was searched, and I was interrogated very harshly for over an hour. I felt like a criminal. I never again travelled to the US for that long, but it didn't end there.

When it was time for my visa to be renewed, instead of getting it like most people without having to go to the embassy, I was requested for an in-person interview with the only available date three months in the future. That was three months of me wondering why I was requested for an interview as they only do that when there is some concern that could lead to you being denied. I have a friend at the gym who was going through something similar. She was also requested for an interview, and she also had the experience in the "room." But her date was almost two months earlier than mine, so she encouraged me to keep checking, which I tried to do daily.

On my way home one evening, I got a text from her that a few earlier dates opened up. Luckily, I remembered the password and quickly logged in to see the dates. I got a date that was just a few days away. My anxiety heightened, though I was relieved that I wouldn't have to wait that long to hear the verdict. I accepted that as a miracle.

The day quickly came, and I went for the interview. I tried my best to maintain my composure, and I was super early that morning. All protocols observed, within a few hours, I was standing in front of a Caucasian consulate who asked me two questions. I am a writer. That is what I do. When is a writer not writing? When I travel, I am working on a book. It is just what I do. I cannot explain the feeling and numbness I felt when this fellow took out the green slip and told me I wasn't qualified for the visa. The reason was, I should not be writing while in the United States because that is considered as me working. I was petrified. Having loaned my wife to this country to work, while I stayed home by myself and endured the agony of being away from my spouse, I was now denied the freedom to go see her.

My wife cried when she heard. It was devastating news. You would think someone had died. But my heart was resilient, and my faith, though reduced to a mere whisper, was still there in the shadows. Between the words I heard from Barbara Oneil (a video my wife sent me) and a call from my mentor, I knew I had to press on. When God closes one door, He opens two other doors. I needed to see beyond the point of disappointment, and only the eyes of faith can see beyond our immediate circumstances. I had no idea how we would process and move beyond that moment, but the clock didn't stop ticking. The news was a devastating start to our year, especially when God told me it was the year of "faith." The expectation was that faith would always produce the desired result, but there is usually a bigger picture that eludes us.

Life is difficult. It is no walk in the park. Our mentality was skewed in the era of the prosperity gospel, where believers started to expect comfort and prosperity. We were taught to drive the best cars, live in the best houses, wear the most expensive suits, etc. While there is nothing inherently wrong with these things if affordable, I choose not to walk that path. The purpose of wealth is to build the kingdom of God, not to inflate our egos.

We must expect difficulties. Paul says:

"For I consider that the sufferings of this present time are not worthy to be compared with the glory that is to be revealed to us." (Romans 8:18 - NASB).

The purpose of faith is not to deliver us from suffering but to take us through it. It takes faith to push through the dross of life, and it may be the only thing that can get us through the challenges and setbacks we face. But if we never go through them, we will never experience what lies beyond. This is why so many believers settle for a mediocre faith life—when things get tough, they give up and settle for the status quo. Settling for what is, however, means missing out on what can be.

There was so much happening when God gave me the title for this book that within a few weeks, I started doubting whether I was even qualified to write it. Fear, worry, anxiety, and defeat crept in. I didn't feel like I was winning in various areas of my life, but God!

Many biblical writers show us the end of their process without divulging the details. When Paul said, **"for I know whom I have believed and am persuaded that He is able to keep what I have committed to Him until that Day." (2 Timothy 1:12b - NKJV)**, he spoke amidst suffering. Statements like these aren't made while standing triumphantly on a mountaintop with hands raised. Faith is most potent and needed in the heat of fierce battles, where our capacity to see beyond dark, dull moments to a glorious light shines through. It is not easy.

Reflecting on my life, I realize I have harvested many unpleasant outcomes from seeds planted in the past. This is how God designed life and time to work—the principle of sowing and reaping. It mirrors how faith operates. Life and circumstances may not change immediately; it is a process. While instantaneous change is possible through belief in the supernatural, it is not typical. Think of faith as a technology—it is really the principle of sowing and reaping. We always reap what we sow. If we sow chaos, we will reap chaos. If we sow bitterness, we will reap bitterness. It is crucial to be mindful of what we plant today because it determines what we cultivate tomorrow—a fundamental principle of change. Change your life now by making better decisions, even if your reality seems unchanged. As time progresses, the seeds you plant will bear fruit, altering outcomes and allowing a different reality to emerge.

It is interesting that the beginning of mankind in Genesis starts with a garden full of fruit trees. Listen to the Word of the Lord:

"Then God said, 'Behold, I have given you every plant yielding seed that is on the surface of all the earth, and every tree which has fruit yielding seed; it shall be food for you; and to every animal of the earth and to every bird of the sky and to everything that moves on the earth which has life, I have given every green plant for food'; and it was so. And God saw all that He had made, and behold, it was very good. And there was evening and there was morning, the sixth day." (Genesis 1:29-31 - NASB).

Adam and Eve had a beautiful beginning. They had access to trees bearing fruit, but they didn't plant those trees. They ate from what God had planted. It gets better:

"Then the Lord God took the man and put him in the Garden of Eden to cultivate it and tend it. The Lord God commanded the man, saying, 'From any tree of the garden you may freely eat; but from the tree of the knowledge of good and evil you shall not eat, for on the day that you eat from it you will certainly die.'" (Genesis 2:15-20 - NASB).

The word "cultivate" is significant. According to bibletools.org:

> *"Adam's job in the Garden was to 'tend and keep' or 'cultivate and guard.' A deeper study of the words shows that in combination, tending or cultivating is a form of keeping. Cultivation is the effort a farmer makes to ensure that he will produce as bountiful a crop as possible. He plows the ground, fertilizes it, plants the seed, then promotes further growth by watering, weeding, and so forth. If the farmer is lazy, if he fails to cultivate his ground, if he does nothing to promote growth, then what occurs? Nature follows its course and the farm begins to degenerate!"*[1]

---

1 https://www.bibletools.org/index.cfm/fuseaction/Topical.show/RTD/cgg/ID/2885/Cultivate-Guard.htm

Man's responsibility was to guard what God had sown to ensure it produced for man's benefit, not God's. And how did all these trees come into existence? They were spoken into existence by God's Word, **"Let there be..."** and there was.

We all have access to a garden on our faith journey where every word we speak is a seed planted. We also have the responsibility to **"tend and keep"** what we sow until it's time to reap the harvest. Why do we see so much chaos in our world today? We can only change the future now by planting seeds that will produce favorable fruit in the future, even if we are not the ones who will eat from the trees.

CHAPTER 7

INACTION ALSO PLANTS FUTURE SEEDS

We were on an excursion to celebrate our anniversary, a few hours' drive from home, when I was stopped by the police. I can't remember what the traffic offense was. I think I got a ticket for not wearing my seatbelt. At the time, the ticket was JA$500. This was a very small sum, even smaller today. I completely forgot about the ticket.

A few years later, I received word that the police were trying to find me. My sister had a friend who worked at the police station, so she called her only to find out there was a warrant out for my arrest. I had no clue what it was about, but I was advised to report to the station the next morning, which I did. It was a Sunday morning, and I was getting ready to go to church. If not for my younger brother, who also had a warrant out for his arrest, I would have spent the night in jail for the first time in my life. The next morning, I reported to the police station and, along with several others, was transported to a courthouse that was hours away in the district where the ticket had been issued. I had to stand before a judge, plead guilty, and pay a fine. Among us was also a pastor who didn't make it to church on Sunday because he was arrested. I barely missed spending a night in jail for a traffic ticket I had neglected.

Sometimes we think that only the things we do have a ripple effect in the future, but our inaction can also produce an undesirable harvest. There is a famous saying: ***"Evil prevails because good men do nothing."***

I believe the ecclesia was given the same measure of power and authority that Jesus displayed in His public ministry. These are His words:

"So Jesus said to them again, 'Peace to you! As the Father has sent Me, I also send you.' And when He had said this, He breathed on them, and said to them, 'Receive the Holy Spirit. If you forgive the sins of any, they are forgiven them; if you retain the sins of any, they are retained.'" (John 20:21-23 - NKJV).

The church is not just the "ecclesia" (called-out ones), but we are also the "sent ones." The scripture spares nothing in informing us of our state as redeemed human beings, and there are some roles that God Himself has not passed on to another:

"And He Himself gave some to be apostles, some prophets, some evangelists, and some pastors and teachers, for the equipping of the saints for the work of ministry, for the edifying of the body of Christ, till we all come to the unity of the faith and of the knowledge of the Son of God, to a perfect man, to the measure of the stature of the fullness of Christ." (Ephesians 4:11-13 - NKJV).

It doesn't matter if we are part of a denomination that no longer believes in these offices; they are not appointments that come from man.

"Most assuredly, I say to you, he who believes in Me, the works that I do he will do also; and greater works than these he will do, because I go to My Father." (John 14:12 - NKJV).

I do not believe we have seen the generation where this prophetic word has manifested. For the most part, the ecclesia is presently struggling to do what Jesus did, so we cannot begin to have a conversation about **"greater works."**

"And I also say to you that you are Peter, and on this rock I will build My church, and the gates of Hades shall not prevail against it." (Matthew 16:18 - NKJV).

Let's put this all into context. If Adam and Eve were created to carry out a certain function in their state of perfection, and they fell from glory, it means the responsibilities they had could not be carried out. Based on the text in Job, we can only assume one of two possibilities: either God assumes the role Himself or He has created beings to carry out those responsibilities until man is once again restored to his original estate. This is what redemption addresses.

We can also assume that God carries out His role perfectly. That has never changed. It means Jesus is building an ecclesia that the gates of Hades cannot prevail over. It also means that Jesus is still appointing Apostles, Prophets, Pastors, Teachers, and Evangelists, because, based on Scripture, all five are needed for us to **"come to the unity of the faith and of the knowledge of the Son of God, to a perfect man, to the measure of the stature of the fullness of Christ,"** as we have discussed in an earlier chapter. It means then that what truncates the effect of the ecclesia in our age and ages past is inaction.

There are many reasons for inaction.

Maybe we have forgotten. We don't remember who we are. Though the Spirit searches the very depths of God and is given to bring us into all truth (specifically about who we are), we are either not paying attention to the infusion of knowledge that is coming, or we are ignoring what we really should know for whatever reason (which is the true definition of ignorance).

Another reason for inaction is a lack of faith. Where there is a lack of faith, we find fear, unbelief, skepticism, and uncertainty, which directly contribute to powerlessness. The danger of this is that our inactions are seeds planted that produce undesirable harvests in our future.

If the ecclesia is unable to heal the sick, it means people will die untimely deaths. It means people will suffer needlessly without relief; it means that purpose, in many cases, will be aborted. The sick often lack the mental fortitude to focus on anything other than the sickness they are going through. Their gifting, calling, and purpose usually take a back seat throughout the course of their suffering. If you have ever been sick, you can relate.

Jesus and His disciples restored many callings, purposes, and divine destinies by changing people's immediate reality. The ecclesia was always meant to continue to do that; to continue that legacy. We literally have everything we need to do what Jesus did, and may I say, the greater works that He mentioned, but we must shed our fear, scrutiny, and hostility towards the process. We must also shed our fear of the unknown because it is impossible to shift to a higher level without abandoning the knowledge of the previous level. There are too many believers who only want to hear what they already know and believe, yet they want to experience something new.

Everything we do now, and do not do, is a seed that is planted. Every seed produces something. Even the very words we speak are seeds.

"Death and life are in the power of the tongue, and those who love it will eat its fruit." (Proverbs 18:21 - NKJV).

Sadly, though we are the sower of seeds, it may not be us who eat the fruits that it bears.

When my wife and I moved into our own home, we had several conversations about fruit trees. We both like the idea of our property being populated with trees from which we can eat. My wife prefers the dwarf version of trees that grow to a reachable height and start bearing fruit in a short space of time. I prefer the real trees that are planted, and we probably have to wait ten years or more before we eat anything from them. They may also grow beyond our reach, but that is still my preference.

"Do not be deceived, God is not mocked; for whatever a man sows, that he will also reap. For he who sows to his flesh will of the flesh reap corruption, but he who sows to the Spirit will of the Spirit reap everlasting life." (Galatians 6:7-8 - NKJV).

I have always been fascinated by the idea that humanity began in a garden surrounded by vegetation and trees bearing fruit. It means our entire existence, even as fallen human beings, is based on the idea of sowing and reaping. We must be intentional about how we live our lives; what we do, and what we say. We must be intentional in doing what God has commissioned us to do, thereby planting good seeds for a future harvest. We must be intentional in speaking what God has ordained us to speak, thereby preparing the fields for a great harvest.

CHAPTER 8

FEAR, THE FAITH-KILLER

It was the year 2012, sometime during the summer, two months after marrying my beautiful wife and one month before my father passed away. I was at home watching a Halloween episode of Law and Order when suddenly, I felt like I couldn't breathe. My youngest sister, brother-in-law, and one of his sisters had just visited and left. I spiraled into a panic I had never experienced before. All I remember was chanting the name of Jesus repeatedly while trying to call my wife. I called her at work, but there was no response. Then, I called my sister, who turned back immediately. I felt like I wouldn't make it through the next few minutes, so I made my way upstairs, still chanting Jesus repeatedly, got dressed, went outside, and closed the door. I wanted to ensure that if I passed out, someone would find me. I was completely engulfed in fear.

When I got outside, one of my neighbors was washing his car. He immediately rushed me to the hospital. I was admitted, and several tests were conducted to determine the extent of my discomfort. My wife, sister, and others met me there and stayed with me through the ordeal. After a few hours, I was told I could go home. The doctor asked me a series of questions and concluded that what I had experienced was a panic attack. That marked the beginning of a decade-long battle with fear.

"Anxiety is the natural result when our hopes are centered on anything short of God and His will for us."[2]

—Billy Graham

The internet provides a vast resource for people with various maladies. No experience or issue is uncommon. Communities and support groups abound for those suffering debilitating effects from anxiety and fear. It became evident that I was not alone but had joined millions facing the same battle. At the core of our struggles lies a legitimate human desire: our desire to live and to be in control.

A single man with little to no responsibility can face fear with courage, but a man who has recently committed himself to a wife, fearing making her a young widow and desiring to live to see a family born of his own flesh, experiences fear differently. Fear and anxiety do not discriminate; they challenge the weak, strong, Christian, and non-Christian alike. For the sake of clarity, fear will be referred to not as a disease, but as Dis-Ease, because it makes life

---

[2] https://billygraham.org/story/how-to-overcome-fear-anxiety-and-worry/

uncomfortable and causes many sleepless nights for those prone to its effects.

Fear first appears in the Bible at the beginning, when man fell (see Genesis 3:10). Before that moment, humanity did not know fear; there was no reason to be afraid. This suggests that fear is a byproduct that entered our context due to the fall, and humanity has suffered from this Dis-Ease ever since. Everything introduced into the world because of sin—I will call "Not-God"—exists as a counterfeit to what is real and true. God created man to have dominion over creation, suggesting some measure of control. There was no disease, sickness, or death; no fatigue, aging as we know it now, or any reason to fear any of those things. When man fell, they lost the capacity to control outcomes, including living and not dying, but the desire to be in control remained. Authors Rachel Starr Thomson, Carolyn Currey, and Mercy Hope, in their book **Fearless: Free in Christ in an Age of Anxiety,** suggest that control is an illusion. They write:

> *"Control can lead to self-destructive behaviors... we try to assert some kind of control when we feel we have none. And the need to control will keep us in fear because we are afraid when we feel out of control."*[3]

[3] Rachel Starr Thomson, Carolyn Currey, and Mercy Hope, Fearless: Free in Christ in an Age of Anxiety (Crystal Beach, ON, Canada: 1:11 Publishing, 2017)

We could differentiate fear and anxiety within separate contexts, but the experience of many suggests a correlation between the two that makes them somewhat inseparable. Anxiety does not exist without fear, and fear does not exist without some measure of anxiety. The Bible refers to fear as a spirit (see 2 Timothy 1:7), suggesting it has a voice. If fear is the voice, then anxiety is the emotional response to those thoughts.

Rita Schiano, a guest blogger on Psychology Today, writes:

> *"As anxiety takes hold, rational decision-making becomes more difficult, and the voice of fear becomes more believable. Rationality is bypassed; what you believe is what matters. And most of the time, what we fear, what we worry about, never materializes."*[4]

Anxiety is considered a complex physiological and psychological state resulting in feelings of apprehension, worry, and unease. Essentially, it manifests as excessive concern about something, usually a phobia of sorts. It is sometimes rooted in a reality that is not yet and may never be, but the mind conjures up worst-case scenarios based on present experiences that are often exaggerated and, in most cases, never occur. Those experiencing anxiety may also suffer restlessness, muscle tension, difficulty concentrating, and various other symptoms that mimic actual illnesses.

---

[4]https://www.psychologytoday.com/us/blog/in-the-face-adversity/201304/fears-connection-anxiety

Anxiety can range from mild to severe and debilitating, and if chronic or overwhelming, it may be classified as an anxiety disorder.

Fear, as many studies reveal, is a basic emotional response to a perceived threat. It is a natural and adaptive reaction that prepares the body to respond to danger, triggering the **"fight or flight"** response with physiological changes such as increased heart rate, heightened alertness, and a surge of adrenaline. It was believed to be a useful condition in ancient times to help humans perceive and escape different levels of threats.

Anxiety makes one uneasy and fuels fear, causing an emotional response to an anticipated threat or outcome that never materializes. Fueling anxiety and fear are our thought processes, or as one author terms it, the **"background noise."** Johnny Cavanos, MD, in his book **Challenge Your Fear, Empower Your Spirit**, writes, *"In 2005, the National Science Foundation published an article summarizing research on human thoughts per day. It was found that the average person has about 12,000 to 60,000 thoughts per day. Of those thousands of thoughts, 80% were negative, and 95% were exactly the same repetitive thoughts as the day before."*[5]

---

[5] https://tlexinstitute.com/how-to-effortlessly-have-more-positive-thoughts

The first battle in overcoming fear and anxiety is gaining control of the mind. Thoughts are real; ignoring them does not benefit us. Psychology attempts to address this Dis-Ease by providing advice outside of a God-response: *"Face your fears and anxieties so they don't become debilitating. Identify ways to create a sense of personal control or mastery in your life."*[6] The Bible offers the God-response (Ref: Philippians 4:8, Proverbs 23:7a, 2 Corinthians 10:5). While we have no control over some things, we have not been relieved of the responsibility to guard and control our thoughts. The biblical approach is to focus only on those things we can control and surrender to God's control.

Fear permeates the Bible from Genesis 3 to the very end. The phrases **"Do not fear," "Do not be afraid,"** and **"Fear not"** appear frequently in scripture as humanity is instructed on how to react to the world beyond the physical. It is easy to base our reality on the visible world, but the unseen realms are marked by uncertainty, the unknown, and endless mystery. The Bible states, **"For when they say, 'Peace and safety!' then sudden destruction comes upon them, as labor pains upon a pregnant woman. And they shall not escape." (1 Thessalonians 5:3).** This means there is always the expectation that trauma, destruction, or some form of calamity may strike at any time—something we cannot control—but we have full control over our response.

---

[6] https://www.takingcharge.csh.umn.edu/how-deal-fear-and-anxiety

When I was in third form in high school, we arrived at class one morning and were having a normal day until two older gentlemen appeared at the door with sad expressions. A classmate, vibrant and showing great potential for a bright future, had suddenly fallen ill and died the previous night. Did he have a choice? Could he have controlled the outcome of his own life? Experiences like these can heighten fear's voice in the form of thoughts like, **"Who's next?"** I remember coming home one night in my late 20s and hearing the news that someone I knew very well, an elderly lady who had just retired, had been murdered. I immediately went inside my room and closed the door and all the windows because I felt I was next.

When God told Adam that if they ate from the Tree of the Knowledge of Good and Evil, they would die, neither he nor Eve had any idea what was coming. They had never seen or experienced death before, so the outcome of their actions was unknown. However, they knew who controlled the outcome. For the first time, they had a Not-God response to their known world, establishing the possibility that a human being could exist in creation based solely on self-response. There are two ways to view this: theological or philosophical.

From a theological perspective, Adam and Eve's disobedience was a turning point in their relationship with God and introduced a self-centered perspective, linked to theological discussions on the consequences of the fall. Philosophically, considerations arise regarding human free will. Philosophers believe in free will and human agency. For instance, existentialist thinkers discussed individuals defining their essence through their choices. Jean-Paul Sartre, in his work "Existentialism is a Humanism," emphasizes existence preceding essence, highlighting individuals' responsibility for their choices.[7]

Because we have a choice, fear and anxiety become issues we battle because we want to control our experiences and outcomes. We fear when we perceive something is going to happen that we do not want. It is believed that at the root of all fears, phobias, and anxieties is the fear of death. In extreme cases, fear of death is named *thanatophobia*[8].

Anxiety disorders are among the most common mental health issues globally. In the last century or so, they have risen exponentially worldwide and are responsible for many Emergency Room visits due to various symptoms. The onset of the COVID-19 pandemic has greatly contributed to the rise in mental health issues across almost all age groups. According to the Centers for Disease Control and Prevention, anxiety disorders often co-occur with depression, affecting over 16 million adults annually in the United States alone.

---

[7] Jean-Paul Sartre, Existentialism is a Humanism

[8]https://my.clevelandclinic.org/health/diseases/22830-thanatophobia-fear-of-death#What%20Causes%20Thanatophobia?

When treating anxiety, growing evidence suggests the most effective approach involves confronting fears while embracing the experience. Many who suffer from fear and anxiety attempt self-analysis, self-diagnosis, and self-medication to alleviate symptoms, but does this address the root problem? We must recognize that fear is a counterfeit of something true and real, such as love and faith (Ref: Romans 14:23b, 1 John 4:18, Romans 8:15, Hebrews 2:15).

The antidote to fear is perfect love and faith, which existed in their purest form before the fall. At the core of **"perfect love"** and **"faith"** is trust in God. The simple truth, though complex in execution and often easier said than done, is to believe God. We must surrender our inherent incapacity to control everything, though we persist in trying. Why? Ultimately, God is in control, and we are in His care. **"For God has not given us a spirit of fear, but of power and of love and of a sound mind." (2 Timothy 1:7 - NKJV).** Fear is Not-God; it is an alternative to Trust-God.

Despite having many preachers in the world today, there is only one place I have heard where anyone can identify that Jesus may have felt fear (Ref: Matthew 26:39). Jesus, knowing what lay ahead, never allowed the future chaos and suffering awaiting Him to prevent Him from living out His purpose and perhaps even enjoying some of life's finer things. He relinquished any attempt to control the future's outcome, and the result— the fruit of the Spirit— was peace.

When Jesus was on a boat with His disciples, while they were gripped by fear of losing their lives, Jesus was sleeping. What gave Him such peace if not the faith He had in the one who controls such outcomes? The fact that Jesus rebuked His disciples for lacking faith despite witnessing His miracles suggests faith would have been the antidote to their fear, and the fruit of that faith would have been peace, even amidst the storm (Ref: John 14:27).

Examining the fruit of the Spirit in Galatians 5:22-23, we find love, peace, and faithfulness as identifiable marks of walking in faith (believing God). A few verses earlier (Galatians 5:13-15), it speaks of love as the fulfillment of the law. The counterfeit would be the works of the flesh (see Galatians 5:19-21), where fear and anxiety lead to idolatry, sorcery (our futile attempts to control outcomes), selfish ambition (a sense of accomplishment from our efforts), and the like. Fear and anxiety hinder us from walking in the Spirit because they are not currencies tradable among children of light (believers).

Someone once said, **"Fear is False Evidence Appearing Real."** It is a type of faith that believes in an outcome that is Not-God. The world is chaotic, and people suffering from PTSD, anxiety disorders, and various phobias experience genuine Dis-Ease. The first step in addressing this from my own experience is acknowledging that God sees what we see and what we do not see. He has a **"bigger picture"** perspective that goes beyond our present experiences. This is the responsibility the church bears. Author Scott

Cormode, in his book **"The Innovative Church,"** questions the relevance of the church today. If the church ignores the issues we presently struggle with, are we truly **"calibrated for a world that no longer exists."**[9]

Fear and Anxiety are issues the church should address in an era calibrated for the age we live in. Fear manifests differently in the lives of believers. Fear of embarrassment or failure can cripple our efforts in fulfilling the Great Commission—thus the ecclesia's mission is hindered by a lack of witnesses. Fear of death can lead us to place greater trust in human attempts to control outcomes rather than in God. Many believers grapple with some form of fear, in all its variations and complexities, making it crucial to address this issue as part of spiritual formation. Jesus' ministry exemplifies that disciples cannot be made without teaching them how to overcome their fears.

Beyond quoting scriptures with a charismatic flair, little emphasis is placed on this debilitating Dis-Ease. I know people who suffer from anxiety and fear and seek external help and resources to address their issues. I would go so far as to say fear can cripple the ecclesia. Fear yields the works of the flesh, but deeper trust and confidence in God yield the fruit of the Spirit. I cannot say I am fully out of the woods as it relates to my battle with fear, but I do know that fear can hamper our capacity to experience the spiritual world. It

---

[9] Scott Cormode, The Innovative Church (Grand Rapids, Michigan: Baker Academic, 2020) pg. 1.

can cause us to see angels as demons, and visitations from God can be perceived as demonic. Fear becomes the most vital spirit to overcome by every believer in order to transition to higher levels of spirituality where our faith becomes even more potent and is not poisoned by Dis-Ease or anything that is Not-God.

CHAPTER 9

FAITH FOR A MENTOR

"When the student is ready, the teacher will appear. When the student is truly ready... the teacher will disappear."

— *Tao Te Ching*

My single life and married life are as different as A.D. and B.C. I struggled as a single man up to my thirty-third birthday to get a commitment from a woman. As a matter of fact, my first real girlfriend was a camp crush in 1996 that lasted for a year. I have never forgotten that girl because I hurt her for a really good friend I was in love with who would never commit to a relationship with me. It is amazing how when you sit to write your memoir, so many details have to be left out so you don't end up with an encyclopedia.

I met my wife in 2010, and we were married on June 02, 2012. It was one of the happiest days of my life, for obvious reasons. I was marrying a beautiful woman whom I thought I never deserved, and I was going to have as much sex as my heart desired. Don't ask if I got all that; I ain't telling. My marriage was a turning point in my life for several reasons. I had been living with my parents up to that point, but I knew that getting married meant I was going to leave and cleave. So, I did just that. For the first time in my life, I was living on my own, and I was the king and priest of my own house.

In September 2012, my father died. He had been sick for some time, but the strangest thing for me was that he died before his eighty-first birthday, which would have been in October. He always told us that the Bible says we live for seventy years and by reason of strength, maybe eighty, but he never believed for more, so he died at eighty. That year, as already mentioned, I also had my first experience of being rushed to a hospital. I was home alone and felt like I wasn't breathing. I was not admitted overnight to the hospital but sent home with a diagnosis of a panic attack. I was also told to look into the possibility of my having sleep apnea. Up until that point, I had no idea what either of those things were, but it started a very interesting journey for me.

The Christian channel TBN was my initiation into the supernatural reality. I had no idea that God was still healing the sick miraculously. The blind were receiving their sight, the mute were speaking, the deaf were hearing, limbs were even growing back, and the dead were being raised. There were some key people whom I followed along their journey, and their testimonies were mind-boggling. I started to read. I got every book I could get my hands on relating to the level of prophetic and supernatural that I was witnessing. I wanted in! Whatever God was doing, I wanted it. I saw it in

Scripture but had never seen it in real life, yet I started to believe for it. I thought that was the ultimate for a believer, but it wasn't.

I started to have some strange spiritual experiences. As I looked back on my life, I realized that was always the case. I had experiences that science calls sleep paralysis, among some other strange occurrences. In piecing it all together, I began to see a spiritual reality that was never taught to me in church growing up. We had a simple take on reality: *if we can see it, it's God; if we cannot see it, it's the devil.* Funny how we thought the devil could prophesy and perform miracles, but the church couldn't. I realized that I needed a mentor because no one could explain my experiences. I remember praying a simple prayer in my heart, *"I would love to be mentored by a Jewish Rabbi."* I found their level of teaching on the Torah to be very profound.

The Jews, even those who have not accepted that the Messiah has come, have a very unique perspective on Scripture. They seem to have insight that unlocks many of the mysteries of Scripture. No wonder the Bible says, **"Salvation is from the Jews."** Their teachings on the Torah, particularly the first five books of the Bible, are remarkable and mind-blowing. I was drawn back to the first three chapters of the Bible, and I got stuck for a long time. I had never really given that section of the Bible much thought, but the more I read, the more it did not make sense to me. What the church teaches about it was equally confusing.

I began to be mentored by authors whom I had never met. I read so many books that I lost count. I was like a sponge absorbing the myriad of knowledge and revelations being recorded in books. I began reaching out to authors whose books deeply resonated with me. Very, very few responded to me, but I remember this one author who sent me a Facebook message. His words were, **"It is well."** I honored this man of God for responding to me, and I started to follow him and his ministry. Prior to meeting him, I also encountered an elderly lady who initiated me into the mystical arena of Christianity. It felt like a much higher dimension of the prophetic, signs, and wonders. Here was a lady with weird, colored hair talking about leaving her body and being taken into heaven. I now have my doubts about her version of heaven, but she helped to prepare me for my mentor and the arena that I was about to be introduced to: **Christian Mysticism.**

Here is a valuable lesson for you: **Have a teachable heart, and God will take you to the depths of His being.** There is a lot that is hidden from us. The Bible calls it **"mystery."** It says that God dwells in thick darkness (see 1 Kings 8:12). He is unknown and shrouded in mystery. What we know about Him is what He wants us to know, but He has many secrets that He reserves for only those who fear Him (see Psalm 25:14). To know God is to fear Him. Here is a Sovereign Being who credits righteousness to the undeserving. In doing so, a Holy God creates a space within Himself for an unholy world filled with unholy people to exist. There are too many arrogant Christians in the kingdom who pretend to be mature and know it all. Their unteachable hearts have locked them out of participating in anything greater than what they already know. I never wanted to be one of those people. I became hungry for knowledge at a very young age. Whatever was trending, I would get all the books I could on the topic and study it. Theology is something I have gravitated towards from a very early age as well. Because my heart is open, even to knowledge that contradicts what I already know, my journey has been quite enlightening.

Meeting my mentor was life-changing. My wife and I obtained our visas and started to travel in 2014. My mother-in-law lives in Prescott Valley, Arizona, so that became our home away from home. We would visit her as often as we could. There was a conference happening at my mentor's church with him and another Christian Mystic as the speakers. When I looked on Google Maps, I realized they were just a six-hour drive away from where we were. I had a crazy thought: book a cheap hotel near the conference location, rent a car, and go to LA. This was the first time we were doing something like that, and it was nerve-wracking. My wife was fully on board.

We stayed in a hotel in Inglewood, CA. When we checked in and got into the room, a cloud of fear enveloped me. I later learned that we had actually stayed in a very bad neighborhood where there were drugs, Mexican cartels, and prostitution. We didn't know that. We even walked freely on the road to go to a supermarket and Walmart. The atmosphere was negatively charged, but I didn't know why. I just felt a sense of doom overtake me, and I wondered what I would tell my mother-in-law if something happened to her only daughter. The weight of responsibility can be overbearing when one is called upon to be accountable. Somehow, God took us through that weekend despite our ignorance.

It was a great experience meeting my mentor and being at a conference with Mystics as the speakers. This opened a whole new world of possibility and divine realities for me. It revolutionized my faith walk. I finally knew what it meant to have faith for the impossible. I finally understood what it meant to have an intimate relationship with the divine. It is nothing like what we practiced in church. Church is about doing; earning your stripes, and working for your heavenly rewards. The path of the Christian Mystic is about becoming. It is experiencing what you know to be true. It is knowing God from the heart and not from the head. **Theology deals with the head, but mysticism deals with the heart.** When you combine them, you have what I call Mystical Theology. This is what is missing in our churches, and until we accept this, we can never truly initiate or cause the transformation our nation is so desperately in need of.

I came upon a saying that I have carried with me since seeing it: *"The Christian of the future will be a mystic, or he will not be a Christian at all."* I believe the traditional church is dying and making way for the church being built by Jesus Himself. It is a supernatural, mystical church that will look very similar to the early ecclesia, bearing the capacity to transform this earth. **We are calling for its destruction, but heaven is rooting for its transmutation.** A new heaven and a new earth are not the absence of the old but a changing from the old to the new. This is what God does with someone who confesses Christ; he or she becomes a new creation.

If everything we have repeatedly done as a church could cause transformation, it would have already taken place. It means then that the change we are crying out for is embedded in what we don't know, which is why we cannot be afraid to explore mysteries.

It is the glory of God to conceal a matter, but the glory of kings is to search out a matter. (Proverbs 25:2 - NKJV).

I now understand the value of mentorship in causing change and also in keeping us accountable. We must believe that God will connect us to the right person. I spent a considerable amount of time trying to find a mentor who would take me under their wing. I needed someone who understood spiritual experiences, but no one wanted the responsibility. Yet, God provided, and some who didn't want to mentor me had a problem with my mentor. Life is funny! We must have a teachable heart in order for us not to miss our divine connections. Understanding that our walk through life is one of faith and that God, our Father, is ordering our steps according to His Word spoken and written about us, then we will be able to identify when our moments of visitation arrive. As it is now, we are unable to identify the Lord or His angels as they come into our presence, as Abraham did.

Then the Lord appeared to him by the terebinth trees of Mamre, as he was sitting in the tent door in the heat of the day. So he lifted his eyes and looked, and behold, three men were standing by him; and when he saw them, he ran from the tent door to meet them, and bowed himself to the ground, and said, "My Lord, if I have now found favor in Your sight, do not pass on by Your servant. Please let a little water be brought, and wash your feet, and rest yourselves under the tree. And I will bring a morsel of bread, that you may refresh your hearts. After that you may pass by, inasmuch as you have come to your servant." They said, "Do as you have said." (Genesis 18:1-5 - NKJV).

We may have had many encounters like these in our own lives but were never able to "see" those encounters for what they really were. We are so enamored by the illusion of the world we "can" see that we miss the movements and interactions of the world we cannot see.

God will always provide what you need, when you need it. He will not allow you to fumble in the darkness with no guidance. When it is time to shift you to higher levels and dimensions of spirituality, God will connect you supernaturally to the right people. In my career as a book publisher, I see each of my clients, even those who are not (yet) believers, as a divine connection. My mentor changed my life, and I am forever indebted to God for allowing me such an honor to be mentored by such a great man of God. Thank you, Dr. O.

CHAPTER 10

BREAKING GENERATIONAL COMPLACENCY

I am the third child of five for my father and the seventh child of nine for my mother. My father had a first wife with whom he had two daughters. She went overseas and never returned, eventually taking their daughters with her. For many years, we maintained contact with them and their children—my nieces and nephews. However, our relationship deteriorated as we transitioned from mail letters to the age of emails and social media. Eventually, they ceased communication with us after my father passed away.

So, I am the firstborn of my father's second marriage. As I write this, my mother is still alive and in her early eighties.

Reflecting on my siblings' lives, I have an older sister who attended teacher's college, which she either self-funded or received funding from someone close to her. When I was younger, I visited her home frequently. Before she became pregnant with her first child, she used to live with us. I am not entirely sure of the arrangement, as her father was not mine, but my father allowed her and one of her other full brothers to stay with us for a while. My younger sister also achieved academically, obtaining a diploma in Business Administration before migrating to Canada. There, she had to repeat a diploma to advance further. None of my other siblings have attended college. It simply wasn't financially feasible for our family, and we all understood that once we graduated high school—if we graduated—our educational pursuits was effectively over. We were largely left to navigate life on our own thereafter.

My own high school performance was lackluster. I didn't realize my potential until a few years after high school. My underachievement wasn't due to distractions such as those prevalent in today's youth, but rather because my father never believed I would amount to anything and I believed him. While perhaps unspoken, his projected belief in my failure was loudly reiterated with each disappointing report card. I distinctly remember collecting a report at the post office that displayed thirteen failing grades out of fourteen subjects. The only subject I passed was Art.

In my final year of high school, I was so consumed by the lack of support and encouragement that would have bolstered my confidence and belief in myself, that I approached final exams with apathy. These exams determined college admission or the prospect of securing a decent job. I was so complacent that I even skipped one of the exams because I heard it was difficult. Consequently, I left high school with nothing. Even my last day at high school was traumatic. Whether through oversight or otherwise, I wasn't chauffeured to school on graduation day. As expected, graduates were required to arrive earlier than the ceremony's scheduled start time. I attended St. Jago High School in Spanish Town, Jamaica. Our family never owned a car, so we relied on public transportation exclusively. It was a 15–20-minute walk from the taxi stand/bus park to my school, a journey I made daily for five years. On graduation day, I only had enough money for a taxi to the usual drop-off point, after which I had to walk the rest of the way to school in my semi-formal attire. Unsurprisingly, I was the only graduate walking along the road to school while others were chauffeured. I can't begin to articulate how that felt; it was a traumatic experience that remains vivid in my mind over thirty years later.

Following high school, my initial jobs included shelf packing at a supermarket, sanding boards for furniture making, and working as a laborer alongside my brother, who was broadening his skill set from carpentry to building contractor. Most of my siblings worked in restaurants, as security guards, or pursued self-taught trades. None of us possessed a business acumen, administrative skills, or money management knowledge, leaving each of us facing a bleak future. Yet, we were largely indifferent to our circumstances.

It took considerable effort to begin believing in myself. For believers, the journey of faith first benefits oneself before it can manifest for God's glory. Often, we harbor grand visions of turning our faith into tangible realities, yet struggle with self-worth, confidence, and comprehending our value from God's perspective. When asked who I am in Christ for the first time, I struggled to find an answer. It was a pivotal moment when I realized that faith must start with self-awareness. We must know who we are and whose we are.

Having grown up in a church culture that heavily emphasizes unworthiness, insignificance, and impurity, my self-esteem suffered greatly. However, as God began revealing my identity in Him, I initially struggled but eventually embraced it, catalyzing a profound shift in my life. It became increasingly evident that I was grappling with inherited challenges from my lineage, which I needed to confront and overcome.

My father lived to be eighty years old. He never believed for more. He consistently voiced this belief while I was growing up that we live to seventy and, by reason of strength, eighty. He never traveled by plane, never obtained a driver's license, never owned a car, and spent nearly thirty years with the same company, leaving behind a pension for my mom that has since diminished in value. He didn't believe in life insurance, seemingly convinced that buying insurance is planning your own funeral. In those days before cell phones, our routine was predictable. If we returned home from school at the same time he returned from work, we would wait at a designated spot for the company bus, which arrived punctually each evening. If he wasn't on the bus, we knew he was working a double shift and wouldn't return until the following morning. Such was life in the 9-5 grind—mundane and predictable.

Upon leaving high school, I took on various jobs, including construction and supermarket employment. I officially entered the workforce at around nineteen years old. My brother, who worked as a "chainman" for a land surveyor, recommended me for a job. The interview, if one could call it that, consisted of a single question: **"Do you eat pork?"** My first employer was a heavy drinker, now deceased. I vividly recall waking at five each morning to meet him and traveling to work in the back of an open van like common laborers. We endured all weather conditions, often arriving at work early and drenched from rain. We endured traffic under the blazing morning sun when he first dropped his daughter at school, forcing an earlier start to my workday. Breakfast and lunch were provided, and pay was inconsistent. I remained with the company for eight years, leaving only after being threatened when frustrations over unpaid wages boiled over. There were countless days spent in that van, driven by an inebriated employer. Only God's protection sustained me during that time, and perhaps extended to others who, like me, were indifferent to God but shared the same harsh conditions.

My second job was with a sober land surveyor, also deceased. My experience there was markedly different, marking my first staff position and the accompanying benefits. My inaugural project involved a segment of Highway2000, a nerve-wracking yet enlightening experience that exposed the inadequacy of my eight years' of field experience. Nevertheless, it proved a valuable opportunity for learning the trade, and I excelled. I expanded my horizons by taking on contract work with other land surveyors.

This led to my third official job as a draughtsman. Initially, my experience with this employer was positive while working part-time. However, upon transitioning to full-time employment, I faced ostracization, shouting, and contempt. It became my briefest tenure at any company since entering the workforce. I had access to my boss's email and witnessed planned indiscretions, revealing deep family troubles. I spent only six months there before moving on.

My final draughtsman position was with a duo of surveyors who had joined forces to establish a company. Unfortunately, I joined them during their impending split, resulting in me working for two separate companies, miles apart. I gradually realized my lack of confidence and inability to assert my beliefs and worth firmly left me vulnerable in the 9-5 environment. I never understood why getting my earned salary required so many meetings, only to discover I was being paid half or less than my true value. After nearly two decades as a senior professional, I departed with nothing—no car, no home, no land, no savings, and in debt. During those years, I began writing and selling plays online, a venture that provided some income. Eventually, I realized my primary job couldn't support itself. The decision to leave was made for me when I arrived at work one day to find someone at my desk performing my duties. My boss insinuated I was slacking off and brought in assistance. I informed him the workload didn't warrant two people, so I left, suggesting he contact me if needed. That was the last time I spoke to him, though I now recognize God's guiding hand over my life, unbeknownst to me at the time.

Becoming an entrepreneur was something I couldn't easily explain to my parents, a reality that persists to this day. My mother often asks, **"Are you still doing what you're doing?"** She remains unfamiliar with my line of work, and there is no way to explain it to her for her to understand. Work for her generation was going outside the home to a place of employment. Anyone who stayed at home was unemployed. Through writing and selling plays online, I earned a four-figure income in USD. Even now, although my business has evolved, many people acquainted with me remain unaware of my occupation beyond book writing. Some might even perceive me as unemployed.

Theological studies always held a special fascination for me. Following high school, while awaiting employment, my days were spent sleeping late, eating, and playing with neighbors, activities curtailed before my father returned home from work. After various odd jobs and completing a carpentry course at HEART, my life remained unremarkable. Please note that I am glossing over these stories, omitting details that warrant their own narrative. I felt out of place during my time at HEART. I would score 19/20 on a spelling test while everyone else just got one word correct. I was the only one in my class who earned the certificate. Despite this achievement, I didn't bother collecting it. I eventually secured that position as a surveying draughtsman, a role about which I initially knew nothing. These were my formative years, during which I began realizing my capacity to excel in any field.

I recall enrolling in Bible courses by mail, frequenting the post office to retrieve modules, mailing completed assignments, and awaiting the next set. For payment, I would visit a bank, obtain a manager's check, and mail it as tuition. This was my introduction to the online environment. My first Amazon purchase involved sending cash in an envelope for an item, an experiment that ended without receiving the product. I completed several Bible courses and enrolled in local options that were available.

When marriage became a prospect, I enrolled in courses through my church, leading to the completion of several theological courses and a diploma from the prestigious Gordon Conwell Theological Seminary based in Boston. They offered reduced rates to members of the Church of God of Prophecy in Jamaica through a consortium arrangement. I embarked on a master's but lost interest and halted my studies. Financial constraints and growing credit with my church's administrative office contributed to my decision, compounded by another issue within our church that will remain unaddressed.

In 2023, the Lord directed me to **"Finish your master's. It's time."** Having suspended studies in 2014, I wondered if I could re-enroll or access the reduced rate independently. Upon contacting the school, within two weeks, I was accepted back into the program to pick up where I had left off. I promptly resumed my theological studies journey. Cultivating a spirit of completion became crucial in my walk of faith. Often, we abandon paths prematurely when trials arise, yet God's promise remains steadfast:

"When you pass through the waters, I will be with you; and through the rivers, they shall not overwhelm you; when you walk through fire you shall not be burned, and the flame shall not consume you." (Isaiah 43:2 - ESV).

Maintaining spiritual tenacity requires not yielding at the first sign of trouble. Challenges will arise, yet God is ever-present. He doesn't compel us forward, but His word stands firm: **"I am with you."**

Growing up in a Pentecostal environment that demonizes the spiritual realm sometimes proves detrimental. I discovered that knowledge often offers greater deliverance than a well-orchestrated exorcism session. Our past or lineage need not define our future, worth, or ability to evolve and influence change. Each of us possesses the potential to make a difference. We overcame adversity from conception through birth to our continued presence here. Perceived limitations are malleable realities. We need not succumb to peer pressure or conform to generational norms. Breaking generational complacency starts with a decision to do so.

Stepping away from the 9-5 structure, establishing my own businesses, and pursuing a diploma or master's degree constituted an uphill battle. I was literally swimming against the tide. I endured the struggle akin to ascending a slope or a treadmill incline. Yet, I persevered, motivated by the envisioned prize. My life seemed destined for failure—a mere statistic of a failed social experiment. However, I unearthed a dormant reservoir within myself and harnessed it to excel in life. This intrinsic capacity resides within all of us, no matter how bleak or insurmountable the situation may appear.

Observing today's teens squandering their lives pursuing the opposite sex and the allure of wealth with minimal effort distresses me. Our generation is ensnared by devices, fixated on the allure of overnight success through viral videos, and fantasizing about living life by our terms with minimal support or accountability. The terms "calling" and "purpose" hold little meaning in this "microwave" generation, fixated on instant gratification. They settle for simplistic pursuits—sex and money—often viewing one as a means to acquire the other. Such pursuits, while straightforward, lack substance. This generation risks failing to tap into their true selves' uniqueness and the latent power within each person. Consequently, many will succumb to generational complacency, thwarting the "greatness" intended for them from birth. For God proclaims:

"For I know the plans I have for you, declares the Lord, plans for welfare and not for evil, to give you a future and a hope." (Jeremiah 29:11 - ESV).

We possess the capacity to dismantle the barriers of failure erected around us by those devoid of hope. We can shatter the shackles of limited expectations imposed by those who fear their own inadequacies being exposed. We can dispel the lies propagated by those who prefer our obscurity, ensuring their comfort remains undisturbed. We can surpass our parents' achievements, a desire any good parent harbors for their offspring. By forging new neural pathways, we cultivate fresh perspectives that foster personal evolution. We can pioneer paths unexplored by previous generations and dare to attempt what they feared. Should opportunities fail to present themselves, we can create them. With belief in our capabilities, the seemingly impossible becomes achievable. Nothing stands beyond reach for those aware of their identity and divine purpose. God is boundless and limitless, dwelling within those who declare Jesus as Lord. Trust in Him and witness the extraordinary unfold, for this is who you are and who you are becoming, though a reality that is not-yet.

CHAPTER 11

FRAMING REALITY

When the Bible says life and death are in the power of the tongue, it isn't kidding.

I grew up in a generation and culture that mostly uses words to frame unwanted realities. It seems the technology of positive speech, affirmations, and declarations falls on deaf ears because there is no taming the tongue. I can use my own life as an example.

For most of my life, I have been overweight. It could be a combination of genes and a very poor diet. I didn't have the knowledge I have today about processed foods, fast foods, etc. In my nation, it is easy to get a nickname based on one's physical disposition, so naturally, those who don't know me would call me "bigs." If you are a woman, it's "fatty." Getting into arguments with anyone would result in degrading terms being thrown at your face, "big, swaughty boi." Of course, "swaughty" isn't even a word, but Jamaicans are known to make up their own words. The meaning is sometimes worse than the words themselves.

It doesn't do much for one's self-esteem when every time someone opens their mouth in your direction, only negativity spews out. My father constantly told me I would never amount to anything. Thankfully, none of his prophetic words came to pass, but it made life really difficult having to press through all that to get to some measure of success. And there is always this feeling of my success being a fleeting reality that could vanish in a moment.

Our words build walls; they create demons. They often frame an undesirable reality that one literally has to go to war with to come out on the other side. This is what we do to each other.

The funny thing for me is, and I will use a more recent observation for this, people will open their mouths to spew out negativity but be silent when the opposite demands it. I decided to grow my hair as I approach my fiftieth birthday. It was a personal choice, as I have tried to mask my age behind a shaved head for over a decade. If I am to embrace who I am and love myself, then I cannot fall for the world's perception of what beauty is. I am fearfully and wonderfully made, even if I am the only one who believes it. I have heard quite a bit of comparison from those who demand that I cut my hair. *"I look old." "I look like a mad person." "I look like Einstein."* I rather like that last one. Why I bring up this example is that I am talking about just a few months of not shaving my head. In over a decade of grooming, I never received one compliment from any of these persons. Never.

This may be a simple example, but it can be much more complex than this. For most of my life, I struggled with my self-image. I hated the way I looked and felt I got the worst end of the stick when it came to physical appearance. I lost my hair on the top of my head, have man "boobs," an overhanging stomach, a missing tooth, discolored skin, enough gray hairs to make me look twenty years older than I am, and a few other things I wouldn't have chosen if I had a say in the matter. People who don't know me think my wife is my daughter when they see us together. Loving myself is a challenge I face, and I am still working my way through it. One of the things the journey of faith forces us to do is to confront the one in the mirror.

As people of faith, we have many tools to shape our reality and the reality of others. These are our thoughts, imagination, emotions, and speech. There must be an agreement between two or more for faith to initiate and create. Many in our time use this faculty for manipulation, some for control, and others for self-service. It would seem that this power of life and death contained within one of the smallest members of our bodies is wasted and used for destruction instead of to build up, edify, and cause transformation.

We are introduced to the power of speech at the beginning of time. We preach it so often: **God said, and it was so.** This same God created human beings who reflected His image and likeness, which means we also have the capacity to speak and see it manifest. The reality we observe through the media and otherwise was framed through our linguistic capacity as humans to create with the spoken word. We have also seen the inability to reframe a new reality because we enforce the present one even further through gossip and fear.

If this world is ever going to change by those who are believers, the language must be addressed. We need to develop a new language based on the reality we desire to see manifested.

Let's examine a Biblical story: the Tower of Babel. Let us examine the words of Yahweh Himself.

"Indeed the people are one and they all have one language, and this is what they begin to do; now nothing that they propose to do will be withheld from them. Come, let Us go down and there confuse their language, that they may not understand one another's speech." (Genesis 11:6-7 – NKJV).

These were not words spoken through prophetic unction, but a direct thought spoken from the one who created all. The people were of one language. The power of unity is not in the gathering under one roof and focusing on one project at a time. It is not in everyone accepting and believing the same doctrinal interpretation, but in speaking one language despite our ethnic, social, racial, and even faith differences. This is the concern I have because with the advent of social media ministries, it is evident that we are all speaking a different language. The mystics bash the conservatives; the conservatives bash the ancients; the Baptists bash the charismatics, etc. It is this "many languages" that has resulted in the fragmentation and disunity of the body of Christ, and may I even say, the world.

Language is so powerful that it can shift a soul from damnation to salvation in a single moment. By confession, a sinner is saved. Language can result in global wars. It resulted in the fall of the human race...*"Did God really say..." "Who told you that you were naked?"* It is more vital how we hear than it is that we can hear. How we hear determines what we see, which influences our perception and shapes our faith.

The language of change/transformation was dismantled at the Tower of Babel. This gave birth to Babylon, which are ancient and present-day systems established and maintained by man to live in creation independent of God; as if that is even possible. It is not bad to unite with one language and do the impossible, but motive is important. Babel wanted to circumvent the rule of God. One writing said that man wanted to ensure that if God decided to flood the earth again, they would have a means of escape. According to God, they were right. It means then that for the world to change, a language needs to be developed that is different from the languages in creation presently.

From a prophetic standpoint, I believe God would allow the world to unite through social media and all these different outlets that have brought us together in a way that we have never been together before. We can have a conference that can be attended by anyone in the world who has access to Wi-Fi without the burden of traveling. The world is experiencing a oneness it has never seen in the history of humanity where we are connected and easily accessible. Now we just need sons to arise and begin to shape this one language that will cause a reformation of creation. This, I believe, is what Isaiah saw when he prophesied that the world would be covered in darkness, but then a great light will appear. This light will expand and cover the earth with the glory of God as the waters cover the sea.

In the interim, we need to practice using the language of life instead of death. Seek to build up instead of tear down. Fight the urge to engage in gossip that plants seeds that bear unwanted fruits in the lives of those we gossip about.

CHAPTER 12

FAITH IS A FREQUENCY

Allow me to be a little scientific in this chapter. I want to examine faith from a scientific perspective. It is a frequency. If it weren't, it could not produce anything.

Everything we know to be physical is a vibration of trillions of cells held together by something. If we should take a human body and pull all the cells apart, the body would disappear. Physicality is energy, frequency, and vibrations. It flows from a macro level that can be seen with the eyes, to a microcosm level, not visible to the human eye. Yet all that is visible is just a compounded effect of that which is not visible.

Faith is an intrinsic component of human spirituality. It is not just a mere belief. It is an ethereal force that connects individuals to a higher power and to each other, akin to a frequency that resonates through the cosmos. Faith operates beyond the physical realm, much like an unseen yet impactful wavelength.

The Bible defines faith in Hebrews 11:1 as **"the substance of things hoped for, the evidence of things not seen."** This verse highlights the dual nature of faith as both a tangible and intangible force. In scientific terms, a frequency is an oscillation or vibration that can be measured, yet often remains invisible to the naked eye. Similarly, faith operates on a plane that goes beyond the physical, manifesting in the tangible world through the outcomes it produces.

The apostle Paul, in his epistle to the Romans, emphasizes the importance of faith in Romans 10:17**: "So then faith comes by hearing, and hearing by the word of God."** This suggests that faith, like a frequency, can be amplified and attuned through exposure to the Word of God. The Word of God acts as a tuner, aligning the believer's heart and mind with the frequency of divine, unchangeable truth. In other words, while it cannot be seen, it is already done.

On closer examination of Genesis 1 and 2, I concluded that God created, but man was charged with the responsibility of manifesting what was created. The very naming of the animals gave them form and function. We learned how important man was in the created space that God established in Genesis 2:

"This is the history of the heavens and the earth when they were created, in the day that the Lord God made the earth and the heavens, before any plant of the field was in the earth and before any herb of the field had grown. For the Lord God had not caused it to rain on the earth,

and there was no man to till the ground; but a mist went up from the earth and watered the whole face of the ground." (Genesis 2:4-6 - NKJV).

Man was not the creator, but he was the sustainer of the created world. His roles included being fruitful, multiplying, and replenishing the earth. The use of the word "replenish" suggests that if or when resources run out, man can replenish them. Jesus alludes to this by turning water into wine and feeding multitudes with seemingly very little. It means that faith as a frequency is also a multiplying principle ensuring that there is no lack, and needed resources do not run out.

In the physical world, resonance occurs when an object vibrates at the same natural frequency as another, causing an amplification of sound or movement. This principle can be applied to faith. When individuals resonate with the frequency of faith, their spiritual and physical realities align with God's will, leading to amplified outcomes. Mark 11:22-24 illustrates this concept through Jesus' teaching on faith: **"So Jesus answered and said to them, 'Have faith in God. For assuredly, I say to you, whoever says to this mountain, "Be removed and be cast into the sea," and does not doubt in his heart, but believes that those things he says will be done, he will have whatever he says.'"** Here, Jesus underscores that faith, free from doubt, can produce miraculous results. This phenomenon is akin to constructive interference in physics, where two waves in phase amplify each other, resulting in a stronger wave. I know there are repetitions throughout this book, but it is necessary to cement in our minds the concept, vitality, necessity, and power of faith.

The Bible frequently highlights the power of words, suggesting that spoken faith can alter realities. Proverbs 18:21 states, **"Death and life are in the power of the tongue, and those who love it will eat its fruit."** This aligns with the concept that frequencies, including those produced by our voice, have the power to influence matter. Just as certain frequencies can shatter glass or heal tissues, the spoken word of faith can bring life or death to circumstances and individuals. This was a profound lesson I had to learn. There is a danger in gossiping and backbiting, which is a common practice among believers today. A mark of a maturing believer is their attempt to control their tongue. Even James alludes to the power of this when he said:

"Even so the tongue is a little member and boasts great things. See how great a forest a little fire kindles! And the tongue is a fire, a world of iniquity. The tongue is so set among our members that it defiles the whole body, and sets on fire the course of nature; and it is set on fire by hell." (James 3:5-6 - NKJV).

Call it a profound sense of humor or just a Father having fun, but God has a way of embedding great power in the smallest of things and making light of what is perceived as larger than life. Consider the giant, Goliath, facing off with a youth carrying a slingshot. The odds were not in the young boy's favor, but by faith, the giant really didn't stand a chance. It takes only a small spark to set a whole forest ablaze. The tongue can do that to one's life, maybe even causing untimely death. I believe so many have been casualties of gossip.

Jesus demonstrated the power of speech when He calmed the storm in Mark 4:39: **"Then He arose and rebuked the wind, and said to the sea, 'Peace, be still!' And the wind ceased and there was a great calm."** His words, spoken with authority and faith, altered the physical reality of the storm, showcasing the transformative power of faith-infused speech.

Faith also operates on a collective frequency, where the combined faith of a community can result in greater manifestations of divine power. Matthew 18:20 states, **"For where two or three are gathered together in My name, I am there in the midst of them."** This verse highlights the principle of collective resonance, where the faith of a group harmonizes, creating a powerful spiritual frequency that invites the presence and intervention of God. Let us not undermine the power of agreement.

"Though one may be overpowered by another, two can withstand him. And a threefold cord is not quickly broken." (Ecclesiastes 4:12 - NKJV).

Acts 2:1-4 provides a vivid example of this collective frequency during the Day of Pentecost: **"When the Day of Pentecost had fully come, they were all with one accord**

in one place. And suddenly there came a sound from heaven, as of a rushing mighty wind, and it filled the whole house where they were sitting. Then there appeared to them divided tongues, as of fire, and one sat upon each of them. And they were all filled with the Holy Spirit and began to speak with other tongues, as the Spirit gave them utterance." The unified faith and expectation of the disciples created a spiritual resonance that facilitated the outpouring of the Holy Spirit. The frequency of faith, when resonated, draws God into our context. It attracts Him to us. Faith is the only thing that can turn God's no into a yes.

"But He answered and said, 'I was not sent except to the lost sheep of the house of Israel.' Then she came and worshiped Him, saying, 'Lord, help me!' But He answered and said, 'It is not good to take the children's bread and throw it to the little dogs.' And she said, 'Yes, Lord, yet even the little dogs eat the crumbs which fall from their masters' table.' Then Jesus answered and said to her, 'O woman, great is your faith! Let it be to you as you desire.' And her daughter was healed from that very hour." (Matthew 15:24-28 - NKJV).

Just as radio receivers must be finely tuned to pick up specific frequencies, believers must attune their hearts and minds to the frequency of faith. This requires intentional spiritual practices such as prayer, meditation on Scripture, and active obedience to God's commandments.

In James 1:6-8, the importance of faith is emphasized: **"But let him ask in faith, with no doubting, for he who doubts is like a wave of the sea driven and tossed by the wind. For let not that man suppose that he will receive anything from the Lord; he is a double-minded man, unstable in all his ways."** Doubt, fear, uncertainty, and unbelief act as interference, disrupting the frequency of faith and preventing the manifestation of God's promises in our lives.

Faith, as described in the Bible, can be likened to a frequency that permeates the spiritual and physical realms. It is a dynamic force that, when properly attuned and amplified, can produce profound effects. Faith is not just an abstract concept but a powerful, resonant force that connects believers to God's will and to each other. By understanding and harnessing this frequency, you can experience the transformative power of faith in your life.

What are you believing God for?

CHAPTER 13

THE WORLD WE LIVE IN TODAY

Babylon is a system designed where humanity learns to live and function in creation without God. Considering the complexities of our modern world, the systems that govern our daily lives often appear to be pillars of stability and progress. Medical, social, financial, religious, and food industries, for example, all appear as essential structures that maintain order and facilitate the functioning of society. But a closer examination reveals a more insidious truth: these systems are reminiscent of the Babylonian empire, a paradigm of control and exploitation. Much like Babylon, our current systems prioritize profit and power over the value of humanity, perpetuating a cycle of dependence and disconnection from our Creator. Since the fall, humanity has always sought a way to perpetuate our existence outside of God, to the point where we now have a vibrant Atheistic movement. It becomes a challenge to talk about faith without measuring its effect and potency in an ever-changing world.

The medical industry is perhaps the most glaring example of a modern Babylonian system. Ostensibly designed to promote health and wellness, it has become a colossal enterprise driven by profit rather than the genuine well-being of individuals. The pharmaceutical industry, in particular, epitomizes this shift. Medications are marketed as miracle cures, but the reality is that they often treat symptoms rather than root causes. This approach ensures a continuous demand for drugs, generating enormous profits for pharmaceutical companies. Moreover, the emphasis on medication over holistic health approaches undermines the body's natural ability to heal and maintain balance. What did we do before there was a pharmacy? What did we do before we had so many doctors and hospitals? Why were we healthier then than we are now?

Presently, I have six bottles of different natural supplements that cost a good penny and are recommended by a naturopathic consultant. It is an alternative to pharmaceutical drugs, but equally, if not more expensive. Yet, the underlying issues faced in the body doesn't seem to regress. In terms of the overall health of the population, why are we getting worse and not better?

A biblical example that mirrors this contemporary issue is the story of King Asa. In 2 Chronicles 16:12, we learn that **"in the thirty-ninth year of his reign, Asa was afflicted with a disease in his feet. Though his disease was severe, even in his illness he did not seek help from the Lord, but only from the physicians."** Asa's reliance solely on human intervention, neglecting to seek divine guidance, ultimately led to his demise. This narrative underscores the folly of placing absolute trust in human systems while ignoring the spiritual dimension of health and healing. So, let's be real. Which one of us is going to have a sharp pain in our chest and go to God first? We are conditioned, by the media and medical professionals, to seek immediate attention, just not from God. So, where we are conscientiously is that human intervention is sought first, and just maybe when we have a surgery to do, or we fill the myriads of prescribed drugs, then we pray for the surgeon's hands that they be steady, and we bless the medication so there is no adverse effect. But have we followed the correct protocols as people of faith? I think you get the point, so let's not belabor this issue.

The social systems in place today also reflect a Babylonian ethos, subtly conditioning individuals to conform and comply. From education to media, the messages we receive often emphasize material success, consumerism, and superficial values. The pressure to conform to societal norms can be overwhelming, leading to a loss of individuality and spiritual emptiness. Social media platforms, for instance, perpetuate a culture of comparison and competition, eroding self-esteem and genuine human connection. These platforms are engineered to maximize user engagement and, consequently, advertising revenue, revealing the profit-driven motives behind their design. In the age of rising "influencers," we get to see the best of worlds. Seldom do we see the real person behind the glitter. There are many who are a **"public success but a private failure,"** as one of my friends would coin it. Yet, we are tempted to measure our own lives and worth based on the perceived reality that we are fed through social media platforms, etc. We have lost the idea of individualism and uniqueness. The question of **"Who am I in Christ?"** gets buried under the aspirations of who we want to become.

Financial systems, too, exhibit characteristics of the Babylonian model, fostering inequality and exploitation. The global banking system, with its complex web of debt and interest, entraps individuals and nations alike. The pursuit of wealth becomes an end in itself, often at the expense of ethical considerations and the well-being of others. The Bible warns against the love of money, stating in 1 Timothy 6:10 that **"the love of money is a root of all kinds of evil."** Yet, our financial institutions thrive on this very principle, creating a society where greed and avarice are not only accepted but encouraged. I am not against wealth.

And you shall remember the Lord your God, for it is He who gives you power to get wealth, that He may establish His covenant which He swore to your fathers, as it is this day. (Deuteronomy 8:18 - NKJV).

Believers should be wealthy, but not through exploitation. We have the power to create wealth through business and investments. Those are the tools the world uses to create wealth and rule the world. Do we go to the ecclesia when we need a mortgage to buy a house or car? While the world accumulates wealth, there are believers embracing poverty as some spiritual virtue depicting humility and grace, but it is nothing more than being lazy.

Religious institutions, which should ideally serve as beacons of spiritual guidance and moral integrity, are not immune to this Babylonian influence. Many have succumbed to the allure of power, wealth, and influence, compromising their core values in the process. The commercialization of religion, where faith is commodified and spiritual leaders wield disproportionate power, mirrors the corruption seen in ancient Babylon. This shift can lead to disillusionment among the faithful, driving a wedge between them and a sincere relationship with God. Without question, the era of the prosperity gospel went way overboard. The main purpose of wealth is to build the kingdom and help to spread the gospel, not accumulate private jets, luxury car collections and indulge in other personal fantasies.

The food industry, too, is emblematic of this systemic control. What we consume is often dictated by profit-driven corporations that prioritize efficiency and profit over health and sustainability. Processed foods, laden with additives and preservatives, dominate our diets, contributing to a host of health issues over time. The industrial farming practices employed to produce these foods often result in environmental degradation, animal cruelty, and a loss of biodiversity. This is starkly contrasted with the biblical vision of stewardship, where humanity is called to care for creation with respect and reverence. From the very beginning, we were given a garden to tend to among all our other diverse responsibilities in creation. Why doesn't every believer have at least a small garden in their homes that they cultivate and tend to? Why are we not planting, replenishing, cultivating, rebuilding, sowing, and reaping? We say we don't have time, but most people I know who don't plant anything find time to binge-watch series on Netflix. Is it a matter of not having time, or is it that our priorities are not in order? I implore you, don't get to the end of this book without planting something.

In essence, the world we live in today is a reflection of the ancient Babylonian system, where human endeavors and institutions are erected in defiance of Godly principles. Faith becomes almost obsolete because we don't need faith to get a car or house; we need a mortgage. We don't need faith to be healed; we need surgeries and drugs. We don't need faith for our next meal; just enough money to load up on processed foods. We have created a world that doesn't need God to function (even though we do because it is His Word that keeps it all together). This systemic disconnection from God leads to various forms of bondage as people become ensnared in cycles of dependence, exploitation, and spiritual impoverishment. There are consequences of such a path, as seen in the story of the Tower of Babel. In Genesis 11:4, humanity's attempt to build a tower **"with its top in the heavens"** was a direct challenge to divine authority, resulting in confusion and dispersion.

To navigate this modern Babylon, a fundamental shift in perspective is required. We must recognize the limitations and inherent flaws of human systems and seek to realign our lives with divine principles. This involves embracing a holistic approach to health that integrates physical, emotional, and spiritual well-being, cultivating genuine human connections, practicing financial stewardship, and advocating for ethical and sustainable practices in all areas of life. By doing so, we can begin to dismantle the Babylonian structures that dominate our world and move towards a society that honors the value of humanity and the sovereignty of God. The call to live in harmony with God's design is a call to resist the seductive allure of Babylonian systems. It is an invitation to seek wisdom and guidance from the Creator, much like the prophets and faithful figures of the Bible who turned to God in times of need. As we strive to embody these principles, we can foster a world that reflects faith, offering hope in a world marred by exploitation and control.

Incorporating a walk of faith in these tumultuous times requires a deliberate and conscious effort to align our lives with Biblical principles, despite the pervasive influence of modern Babylonian systems. There are several ways we can do this in today's challenging environment. Firstly, and probably most importantly, we need to prioritize spiritual practices. Yes, your grandma was right when she said, *"Read your Bible and pray"* when you are having issues. I remember the first time I made up my mind to read the Bible from Genesis to Revelation. It took me a whole year, but it changed my life. I subsequently took up leadership positions at church, became a minister in training, and led the Bible Study team. It is amazing what the written Word of God does to your heart and mind just by reading it. Imagine what it can do if you study it.

Spiritual practices include prayer (not just audible, but contemplative), meditation, reading and studying scripture, fellowship with one another, and communion. Spiritual practices ground us in our faith and open up a line of communication between us and God. It helps bring us in alignment with the seven spirits of God:

The Spirit of the Lord shall rest upon Him, the Spirit of wisdom and understanding, the Spirit of counsel and might, the Spirit of knowledge and of the fear of the Lord. (Isaiah 11:2 - NKJV).

And to the angel of the church in Sardis write, 'These things says He who has the seven Spirits of God and the seven stars: "I know your works, that you have a name that you are alive, but you are dead."' (Revelation 3:1 - NKJV).

Through practice, we learn to approach life with wisdom and discernment. The Bible encourages this in 1 Thessalonians 5:17, which says, **"Pray without ceasing,"** emphasizing the importance of maintaining a continuous connection and communion with God.

Additionally, we also need the support of our faith community—the ecclesia. There is no spiritual growth for the believer in isolation. Our Creator made this clear when He said: **"It is not good that man should be alone;" (Genesis 2:18 - NKJV).** Perceived isolation is the world's downfall because we fail to see how much we need each other. Whether through a local church, small group, or online fellowship, being part of a community of believers provides encouragement, accountability, and shared wisdom. Hebrews 10:24-25 highlights this, stating, **"And let us consider how we may spur one another on toward love and good deeds, not giving up meeting together, as some are in the habit of doing, but encouraging one another—and all the more as you see the Day approaching."**

I used to practice downloading movies and music through what was known as "torrents." It is a form of bootlegging where we escape having to pay for something to gain access to it. One day, the Lord said to me, ***"Maintain the integrity of your soul, and all will be well."*** This is the practice of ethical living; it is how we conduct ourselves when no one is looking. Our actions must align with our beliefs by living ethically and justly. This involves making choices that reflect our faith, such as supporting fair trade, reducing consumption, and advocating for social justice. Micah 6:8 calls us to **"act justly and to love mercy and to walk humbly with your God,"** reminding us of the importance of living out our faith through our actions, especially when no one is looking.

The next thing we must consider is taking a holistic health approach by integrating physical, emotional, and spiritual well-being. This includes seeking natural and preventive healthcare methods, nourishing your body with wholesome foods, exercising consistently, and addressing mental health issues with compassion and care. The Apostle Paul reminds us in 1 Corinthians 6:19-20 that our bodies are temples of the Holy Spirit, and we should honor God with our bodies. One of the hardest things I have had to do in life is to start exercising. I used to weigh close to 350 pounds and was living a rather sedentary lifestyle. When I became an entrepreneur, I spent most of my days sitting at a desk. At the time, I was also consuming a lot of processed and fast food. One day, out of nowhere, the Lord said, ***"Do some push-ups."*** I was taken aback initially by the request, but reluctantly, I went down to the floor, hands spread, elbows up and attempted to push myself off the floor. I couldn't budge my body by even a centimeter. That was when I realized I was at a very bad place.

I found the nearest gym—about 30-40 minutes' drive—and I went and started a membership with personal training. On day one, I was put on what is called a "lazy bicycle" for fifteen minutes. The entire world started spinning. To this day, I don't know how I made it to the car and drove myself home. I crashed in bed for a while before I was myself again. That started me on a new journey of finding health and vitality and changing my diet. I believe that little, subtle request from God may be the reason I am still here. I have subsequently developed a deep passion for longevity, and I am in search of the fountain of youth or the elixir of life.

In the advent of COVID-19, there was a saying that was coined in addition to all the protocols that were put in place, ***"Your health, Your responsibility."*** We live in an age where we want to do what we want, eat what we want, think what we want, and when something goes awry, we seek for someone or a magic pill to make it better. There is a greater call on our lives to assume personal responsibility for our health and well-being.

Exercise discernment in the media you consume. Much of modern media perpetuates values that are contrary to faith, such as materialism, violence, and immorality. Addiction to porn is more common than we know and often requires professional or divine intervention to break the habit. By being selective about what we watch, read, and listen to, we can protect our minds and hearts from negative influences. I find that we really don't pay much attention to this in our day. Philippians 4:8 encourages us to focus on what is true, noble, right, pure, lovely, and admirable.

Practice financial stewardship by managing your resources wisely and generously. This means budgeting carefully, avoiding debt, and giving to those in need. Jesus taught in Matthew 6:19-21, **"Do not store up for yourselves treasures on earth, where moths and vermin destroy, and where thieves break in and steal. But store up for yourselves treasures in heaven... For where your treasure**

is, there your heart will be also." One of the greatest investments we can make is in people. They are made in the image and likeness of God. This is one way to store up treasures that are unaffected by decay. Our financial choices should reflect our eternal priorities.

Commit to continuous learning and personal growth in your faith. Attend Bible studies, read theological books, and seek mentorship from mature Christians. 2 Timothy 2:15 encourages us to **"Do your best to present yourself to God as one approved, a worker who does not need to be ashamed and who correctly handles the word of truth."** Find balance and rest in your life. The relentless pace of modern society can lead to burnout and spiritual exhaustion. Observing a Sabbath rest and taking time to rejuvenate is essential. Jesus said in Matthew 11:28-30, **"Come to me, all you who are weary and burdened, and I will give you rest... For my yoke is easy and my burden is light."**

Developing faith in our modern context must be the goal of the believer. Ultimately, we must learn to trust in God's sovereignty and plan for our lives. Amidst the uncertainties and challenges of these times, remember that God is in control. By incorporating these principles into our daily lives, we can walk in faith even amidst the turbulence and influence of modern society. This journey requires intentionality, perseverance, and a steadfast commitment to living out our faith in every aspect of life, trusting that God will guide and sustain us through all challenges.

CHAPTER 14

FAITH FOR PROTECTION

The angel of the Lord encamps all around those who fear Him, and delivers them. (Psalm 34:7 - NKJV).

We don't always see the hand of God in our lives unless we are standing on the event horizon looking back. In the moment, I am often too filled with anxiety to see God working or even to hear Him speaking. This is something I need to keep working on.

I remember years ago, my best friend asked me to drive her car to the market in Kingston. I was learning to drive at the time and eagerly took every opportunity to practice. We parked at Coronation Market, just opposite the police station. I wasn't thinking about any potential risks that day. I don't even remember where my mind was wandering. So when a guy suspiciously stood at the back of a nearby van and glanced momentarily in my direction, I dismissed it. I sat in the car, having breakfast, while my friend and her colleague went to the market.

The Bible says:

"For when they say, 'Peace and safety!' then sudden destruction comes upon them, as labor pains upon a pregnant woman. And they shall not escape." (1 Thessalonians 5:3 - NKJV).

It is not that we should respond to life with anxiety, worry, and agitation. It speaks more to being vigilant in an unpredictable and uncertain world. The moment we let our guard down and start to walk through life like zombies, unaware and unconscious, something usually happens to shock us back to reality. That's just how life is designed. Human beings were made to live with intentionality and purpose.

When my friend returned to the car with the market goods, we loaded up and prepared to leave. As I closed the door, it suddenly stopped just short of closing completely. I turned and saw a man stooping down at the door with a long gun in his hand. *"If you move, me shoot you,"* he said. I heard the words, but the world seemed to stop moving. My ears rang, and my mind went blank and dark, like in a dream.

I was ordered to the passenger side, and another guy took the driver's seat. I wasn't sure if he had a gun. The one I saw with a gun sat behind me, and they drove off with me still in the car, head bowed, completely uncertain how that morning would end. My life didn't flash before my eyes, but I wondered what it would feel like to be shot in the head.

As they drove down the road and turned onto an isolated street, they stopped, and I was ordered out of the vehicle. I remember saying *"Thank you,"* but not to them – to a higher power that deemed me worthy to live and not become a casualty in a war I didn't sign up for. We lost the car, but our lives were spared.

Fast forward to a more recent event: I was traveling on a long, straight road heading into Portmore, St. Catherine. I was behind a van following a truck that was moving very slowly. I think the truck driver sensed something was wrong from the speed he was going. We knew something was wrong because we could smell burning rubber.

Life can change in a moment, in the twinkling of an eye. The Bible speaks of a future event in a similar way:

"In a moment, in the twinkling of an eye, at the last trumpet. For the trumpet will sound, and the dead will be raised incorruptible, and we shall be changed." (1 Corinthians 15:52 - NKJV).

I find the language of scripture very interesting. I don't think it is just about a moment in time, but the unexpected occurrence will seem to happen so fast and suddenly. This entire transformation will happen simultaneously, seemingly in just a moment, and so it is for us today. Many woke up fine, had a bath, ate a good breakfast, got dressed, and left home, only to have their lives severely altered in an instant. I have a cousin who left his house one Sunday evening to deliver something in Kingston and never made it back home. The next time anyone saw him, he was lying in a morgue because a stray bullet hit his heart while he stopped at a stoplight. To this day, no one really knows what happened.

So, in a moment, I saw one of the wheels on the truck come off. Strangely, it seemed as if someone controlled the wheel as it rolled backward, passed behind the truck, and crossed into oncoming traffic. A van leading a line of traffic on the opposite side took the full impact of the wheel head-on. I saw his front end shatter, debris flying in different directions, but I also saw the wheel heading towards me. There was no time to think or maneuver; only God could have caused that huge wheel to hit my car in a way that resulted in minimal damage. I am certain an angel steered that wheel clear of causing major harm. This was days before I sold that car.

If you allow yourself to stand on the event horizon (that place in your mind where you can look back with absolute clarity), you will see that you have greater testimonies of God's providence than just saying *"Amazing Grace, how sweet the sound."*

"Blessed shall you be when you come in, and blessed shall you be when you go out." (Deuteronomy 28:6 - NKJV).

Our days don't always go as planned, but we often don't see how much worse things could have been had God not ordered our steps. This is the danger of ingratitude. We miss those divine moments when God shielded us from major catastrophes, allowing only minor incidents to occur. In all things, we should give thanks, for this is the will of God in Christ.

Angels are assigned to those who are heirs of salvation. They are activated in and around us to help us navigate each day. Dangers lurk around every corner. Life can sometimes feel like a scene from Final Destination, and for some people, it is or was, but God. If I have learned anything on this faith journey, it is this: God sees, God knows, and God acts on my behalf – always. Trust Him. He watches us closely because we belong to Him, and He guides our experiences so they never exceed what we can bear. It is always within reason and just enough to avoid destroying us.

CHAPTER 15

FAITH WITHOUT WORKS IS DEAD

The writer of Hebrews states quite succinctly: **"But without faith it is impossible to please him: for he that cometh to God must believe that he is, and that he is a rewarder of them that diligently seek him. (Hebrews 11:6 - KJV)."** The use of the word **"impossible"** in that text is quite telling. It means that faith becomes the quintessential quality in the life of the believer. Without faith, there is no way for a human being to please God. If God cannot be pleased except by faith, then we can conclude that it is impossible to please God without the corresponding **"works"** related to faith.

"Faith Without Works is Dead" is adopted from the idea presented by Apostle James' writings where he states in writing to the twelve tribes of Israel: **"But do you want to know, O foolish man, that faith without works is dead? Was not Abraham our father justified by works when he offered Isaac his son on the altar? Do you see that faith was working together with his works, and by works faith was made perfect?" (James 2:20-23).**

Faith independent of works is imperfect and incomplete. Theology is essentially the study of God in relation to humanity. We know that God is a triune God: Father, Son, Holy Spirit. In Scripture, we see Jesus praying to the Father, then sending the Holy Spirit after He ascended. Each plays a unique and specific role, yet they are one. There is a mystery here that is hard to articulate, but considering that the human being is also triune: body, soul, and spirit, then that becomes a starting point in understanding the trinitarian reality of the Godhead. We are body, soul, and spirit, but one person. God is Father, Son, and Holy Spirit, but one person.

Christianity is the path chosen by those who accept Jesus as Lord and Saviour, recognizing that He is the Way, Truth, and Life. Christians are often referred to as **"Believers"** or **"People of faith."** So, the question is asked, is faith passive? Or is faith active?

There is an ongoing debate as to what the church should look like today, and theologians have drawn different conclusions. There are different approaches to theology, two are of particular interest to me: the Theologies of Transformation and the Theologies of Escape. The concept of these approaches is good, but it puts the fully manifested realities of our faith somewhere in the future. The idea of **"transformation"** puts the full manifestation of the kingdom of God in the future, which makes hope an attribute to access that reality via perception in order to live in the present age. The idea of **"escape"** is that believers should not be relegated to experiencing any level of persecution or tribulation, but God will make a way of escape for those who belong to Him. In both cases, I believe, the concept of faith is somewhat diminished because while faith is needed to accept these future realities, it does very little to influence or change our present realities. Any conclusion we draw must relate somehow to the idea of **"salvation"** and what it means for us as born-again believers.

The most important Hebrew root word related to salvation in the Old Testament is *yasha*. Originally it meant to be roomy or broad in contrast to narrowness or oppression. Thus, it signifies freedom from what binds or restricts, and it came to mean deliverance, liberation, or giving width and breadth to something—Faith was the necessary condition for salvation in the Old Testament as well as in the New. Abraham believed in the Lord, and the Lord counted it to him for righteousness (see Genesis 15:6).[10]

One consensus on salvation is that it is both instantaneous and progressive. We are told to **"work out your own salvation with fear and trembling."** (see Philippians 2:12). On the matter of faith that produces both salvation and the corresponding works that make it alive and not dead, there is one scripture we can contemplate: **"He who believes and is baptized will be saved; but he who does not believe will be condemned. And these signs will follow those who believe: In My name they will cast out demons; they will**

[10] Charles Caldwell Ryrie, Basic Theology (Chicago, Ill.: Moody Press, 1999), 321.

speak with new tongues; they will take up serpents; and if they drink anything deadly, it will by no means hurt them; they will lay hands on the sick, and they will recover." (Mark 16:16-18 - NKJV).

Faith requires us to do something and is not sufficient in and of itself. We believe to be saved, but to produce the works, we must act on our faith. **Jesus answered and said unto them, "This is the work of God, that ye believe on him whom he hath sent." (John 6:29 - KJV).**

One of my professors, in talking about the theologies of escape, mentioned the conflict that exists between faith and the continuation of faith. In my own culture, it is often said about certain actions and beliefs that **"those have no bearing on our immediate salvation."** In other words, believing in Jesus is sufficient without having to perform any works in relation to our faith to validate our position as a believer. But the book of Hebrews raises other concerns: **"Therefore, leaving the discussion of the elementary principles of Christ, let us go on to perfection, not laying again the foundation of repentance from dead works and of faith toward God." (Hebrews 6:1 - NKJV).**

The original word used for **"faith"** in James 2:20 is ***"pistin"*** which means faith, belief, trust, confidence, fidelity, faithfulness. The word used for **"works"** is ***"ergon,"*** meaning toil, by implication, an act. It is the same words used in Hebrews, so connecting the text in James to Hebrews will conclude that **"dead works"** flow from immaturity as a believer, suggesting that **"dead works"** refers to faith that does not produce a corresponding action that validates its reality.

Salvation only became a necessity because man fell (see Genesis 3). Faith is the technology by which we access this salvation in its present continuous tense. For as by one man's disobedience many were made sinners, so by the obedience of one shall many be made righteous (see Romans 5:19 - KJV).

Only a man without sin could redeem man from his fallen state. Since by virtue of the fall, there was no man that could be found who had no sin, such a predicament could only be solved by our Creator taking on the form of a human being. Therefore, salvation is made available to all people, but it can only be accessed by an act of one's will by faith. Faith becomes the magnet that draws unseen realities into our context enough to produce a new reality for the one who believes. For example, a human being on his way to eternal damnation can change course by acting in faith in Jesus and choosing to follow the path of salvation, thereby changing his eternal course completely. We see many examples of this outworking of faith in Scripture that can shift even the most dire of circumstances and change a person's narrative. On several occasions, Jesus is quoted as having said, **"your faith has made you well."** (Ref: Matthew 9:22, Mark 5:24, Luke 8:48, Luke 17:19).

Faith then has the power to change outcomes, not just in a future context but in present realities. However, faith requires a corresponding action to activate its fullest potential and draw realities from the unseen into the seen realm. We know we have faith because we are people of faith, but does it provoke us to act? If God instructs, are we willing to walk into our local morgue and try to raise someone from the dead? Are we willing to tell a lame man in a public space, ***"Get up and walk?"*** Will we risk embarrassment and possibly public ridicule to act on our faith in an attempt to produce a contrasting reality? Is God not searching for the man or woman who will risk everything to be obedient to His voice? The ecclesia has lost this culture, and it must be restored if we are going to be the radiant and glorious church referenced in the book of Ephesians.

Faith, in its passive sense, is safe and provides a comfortable space where the believer can live somewhat of a normal life in the eyes of the world, but such faith is dead because it doesn't produce anything but salvation. We create converts and church-goers, but not disciples and witnesses of the manifested power of God. Paul says:

And my speech and my preaching were not with persuasive words of human wisdom, but in demonstration of the Spirit and of power, that your faith should not be in the wisdom of men but in the power of God. (1 Corinthians 2:4-5 - NKJV).

The ecclesia should be able to make this statement as well. Passive faith doesn't change realities or shift outcomes. It doesn't threaten the world's status quo or assuage the effects of the kingdom of darkness. Faith is activated when it is acted upon. If we do nothing with our faith, then it is dead.

CHAPTER 16

LITTLE FAITH

"But He said to them, 'Why are you fearful, O you of little faith?' Then He arose and rebuked the winds and the sea, and there was a great calm." (Matthew 8:26 - NKJV).

We know this story well. The disciples were on a boat in the sea when a violent wind came up against them. As we would be, they were fearful for their lives, and they found Jesus sleeping. Initially, they perceived that maybe He didn't care whether they perished or not, but Jesus saw through their fear to the real issue at hand: they had little faith. Little faith gives way to a fearful response when we face storms in life, and fear allows faith-killing thoughts to invade our minds.

What I love about this story is that Jesus alluded to the fact that His trusted companions did not have to wake Him. What He was about to do, He also knew they possessed the power to do. Does fear blind us to the truth of who we are and what we carry? Jesus spoke to the wind, and it immediately obeyed.

"And immediately Jesus stretched out His hand and caught him, and said to him, 'O you of little faith, why did you doubt?'" (Matthew 14:31 - NKJV).

Simon Peter is special among Jesus' followers. Without question, when Jesus told him to follow, Peter did not hesitate. Later, we learned that he had a family (wife, mother-in-law). The price he paid to follow Jesus was high, and we can only hope that his life resembled what we see in the series **"The Chosen,"** not a complete abandonment of his responsibilities as a husband.

There is something about water in relation to Jesus' ministry. His first miracle was turning water into wine, and some of His greatest demonstrations of power over creation happened on water. Again, the disciples found themselves in a precarious position: out at sea, and a violent wind came against them once more. But this time, Jesus was not on the boat. Momentarily, they saw Him walking towards them on the water. Peter was the only disciple who saw an opportunity and took it.

"And Peter answered Him and said, 'Lord, if it is You, command me to come to You on the water.' So He said, 'Come.' And when Peter had come down out of the boat, he walked on the water to go to Jesus. But when he saw

that the wind was boisterous, he was afraid; and beginning to sink, he cried out, saying, 'Lord, save me!'" (Matthew 14:28-30 - NKJV).

Many preachers focus on Peter taking his eyes off Jesus and beginning to sink, prompting Jesus to stretch out His hand and save him. What fascinates me, however, is the fact that Peter actually took a few steps on water, which is **"impossible"** for a mere man…or is it?

Jesus attributed Peter's dilemma to having **"little faith."**

"If then God so clothes the grass, which today is in the field and tomorrow is thrown into the oven, how much more will He clothe you, O you of little faith?" (Luke 12:28 - NKJV).

One of the earliest revelations of God's divine attributes is **"Jehovah Jireh."** He is Provider. If God can take care of that which is not conscious of being taken care of (i.e., the plant and bird life), how much more will He take care of us, who are His children and heirs of His magnificent kingdom? It is amazing that we can doubt God's ability to provide in the midst of our seasons of need to the point where worry consumes our minds. In a sense, our capacity to worry and experience anxiety is linked to having **"little faith."** I know this posture very well. It essentially declares that we don't believe God will act for us, for whatever reason.

I once heard someone say that God wants to heal us more than we want to be healed. I found that hard to believe in an era when a great number of the population is on some form of pharmaceutical drugs for some ailment with little to no relief. If God wanted to heal us more than we wanted to be healed, why are we even sick to begin with?

"But without faith it is impossible to please Him, for he who comes to God must believe that He is, and that He is a rewarder of those who diligently seek Him." (Hebrews 11:6 - NKJV).

It amazes me the power that faith has to change realities. One can be on their way to hell, and through repentance and confession, make a complete turnaround and now be on their way to paradise.

By faith, we see nature responding to the voice of a man. By faith, we see men walking on water. By faith, we know supernatural provisions have been made. Jesus fed 5000 men (not counting women and children) with five loaves and two fish. Is it even remotely possible that we can accomplish these same feats if only we had enough faith? But how much is enough faith?

"And the apostles said to the Lord, 'Increase our faith.' So the Lord said, 'If you have faith as a mustard seed, you can say to this mulberry tree, 'Be pulled up by the

roots and be planted in the sea,' and it would obey you.'" (Luke 17:5-6 - NKJV).

The problem is not that our faith needs to increase, but there needs to be the absence of something that congeals or totally renders our faith worthless.

"Then Jesus answered and said, 'O faithless and perverse generation, how long shall I be with you? How long shall I bear with you? Bring him here to Me.' And Jesus rebuked the demon, and it came out of him; and the child was cured from that very hour. Then the disciples came to Jesus privately and said, 'Why could we not cast it out?' So Jesus said to them, 'Because of your unbelief; for assuredly, I say to you, if you have faith as a mustard seed, you will say to this mountain, 'Move from here to there,' and it will move; and nothing will be impossible for you. However, this kind does not go out except by prayer and fasting.'" (Matthew 17:17-21 - NKJV).

Where there is doubt, there can be no miracle because faith is the absolute confidence that what you are believing for will be done. Our measure of faith is enough. A mustard seed is one of the smallest seeds in existence. What produces miracles is the absence of doubt and uncertainty. We must know without a shadow of a doubt that God will perform His Word when spoken. **If God has said it, it is a done deal.**

Little Faith

Grow your confidence by practicing your faith, regardless of how little you perceive it to be.

CHAPTER 17

GREAT FAITH

I have had quite a few profound spiritual experiences that are hard to explain or even relate to sometimes. My church was usually within walking distance of where I lived. So, usually, when I was having a difficult season, I would often walk to the church and sit silently in the dark while my mind tried to process whatever I was going through. This was somewhat of a regular practice, as being on the church grounds usually brings some measure of calm and peace.

One day, I was at church by myself when I felt something come into me. The only way I can describe it was it felt like a sword was pushed into one side and it came out on the other side. I still don't know what happened or what it meant, but I felt relief from what I was experiencing at the time. I realize that such spiritual experiences can often precede a coming difficult season. In a sense, it is God's way of preparing us for what's to come. Accept this as encouragement; **before a storm, our Father takes us through a period of preparation.**

On another occasion, I was home alone, I believe, when I felt a spirit enter me. Now, most Pentecostals demonize the spiritual realm to their own detriment, but my journey has taught me to make distinctions. As a believer, God interacts with us more than the demonic realm. I find it funny that even in my church, we can talk about demons freely, but any mention of angels needs explanation and biblical backing. I perceived that when that spirit entered me, it was the spirit of faith. My faith, in that moment, was heightened to a level I had never experienced before. I suddenly felt like nothing was impossible, and anything I desired would be granted. That was preparation for some difficult seasons that were coming.

Great faith will always be tested. It is not something granted for us to get riches to splurge on our personal desires and fantasies, but it is a cementing of our trust in God, despite what we are going through. On several occasions, the disciples are judged for having **"little faith"** when faced with a storm. How we respond to the storms of life is a determining factor of our level of faith. Are we able to see beyond the chaos, beyond the debilitating symptoms, beyond any dark, perceived reality, and see the God who exists above it?

Yet in all these things we are more than conquerors through Him who loved us. (Romans 8:37 - NKJV)

I have learned that life is not a walk in paradise; it provides opportunities for us to overcome. It is the process by which we go through to reveal a greater glory.

The elders who are among you I exhort, I who am a fellow elder and a witness of the sufferings of Christ, and also a partaker of the glory that will be revealed: (1 Peter 5:1 - NKJV)

For I consider that the sufferings of this present time are not worthy to be compared with the glory which shall be revealed in us. (Romans 8:18 - NKJV)

I often tell people that life is difficult, and indeed it is. We can have good seasons and find ourselves in a good place where we are happy and content and there is no trauma in sight, when suddenly something happens to turn our world upside down. That is the nature of life, and I question the reason for it all. I have come to learn that because of the fall, we must go through a process to eradicate the very nature of that fall in order to reveal the greater glory in us that we fell short of. It is a process as the elements of gold must be tried by fire in order to reveal its true nature and value. Each test that we overcome increases our faith by a measure because it cements the fact that if we went through it and came out on the other side, then the God who brought us through can do it again.

I shared this story already in a previous chapter, but I want to share it again. My wife was overseas working. I was visiting with my mother-in-law, so I was almost 3000 miles from where my wife was at the time. Her cousin was studying abroad for two years, and they bought her an old car to aid with her daily traveling. Her cousin had finished studying and was returning home, so there was a conversation regarding the car and what to do with it. It was old, so it had very little value, and no one knew the process to go through to get it sold. My wife needed a car for work, so it was decided to pass the car on to her, but how would she get it? Someone needed to drive the car to her; I volunteered. Now, understand that driving overseas is very different from what I was used to back home because they drive on the wrong side of the road. Consider also that I had never driven more than six hours in the United States, and that was nerve-wracking. So here I was, about to embark on a 40-hour drive across several states in the United States in an old car in the winter.

When I woke that morning, I realized the car had a small oil leak. I mustered up all the faith I could find to get into that car and begin my journey. It was indeed a learning experience. I chose to take roads that had no tolls, not knowing I would be traveling on some lonely back roads, with huge trucks and limited lighting. It was a four-day trip, stopping at gas stations as a black man in strange places, getting food in places where there were no black people in sight, and staying in hotels in unknown places. I was afraid, but I did it afraid.

Having faith is not always about being fearless, but great faith allows us to learn to **"do it afraid."** I have done that 40-hour drive several times after that, and each time was a brand-new experience. What carried me is God's Word that **"I can do all things…"**

Then Jesus went with them. And when He was already not far from the house, the centurion sent friends to Him, saying to Him, "Lord, do not trouble Yourself, for I am not worthy that You should enter under my roof. Therefore I did not even think myself worthy to come to You. But say the word, and my servant will be healed. For I also am a man placed under authority, having soldiers under me. And I say to one, 'Go,' and he goes; and to another, 'Come,' and he comes; and to my servant, 'Do this,' and he does it." When Jesus heard these things, He marveled at him, and turned around and said to the crowd that followed Him, "I say to you, I have not found such great faith, not even in Israel!" (Luke 7:6-9 - NKJV).

Believing in Jesus' capacity to speak and seeing it manifest is the qualifying principle of great faith. This is our challenge today. We have the written Word of God, which is the spoken Word of God, at our fingertips, but we struggle to believe what it says. We often believe it either doesn't apply to us in context, or we just don't have enough faith to see beyond our immediate circumstance to embrace a different reality. **We cannot see unless we believe, and we can only see what we believe.**

For many years, I struggled because of indoctrination. I grew up in a church culture that greatly emphasized the idea of a **"rapture"**—that Jesus would come any minute now. It caused me to struggle with doing anything that would take years. So, I never prioritized healthy living, exercise, or education because these were long-term goals. So when I got a chance to start my Masters in Theological Studies, I didn't take it as seriously as I should. If I did, I would have accomplished my PhD by the writing of this book. I lagged behind because even though I have relearned the whole concept of **"occupy until I return,"** the old teachings were still ingrained in my consciousness, so anything long-term seemed like a waste of time.

In 2023, God told me to finish what I started. I had stopped my masters in 2014; that was over eight years. But it wasn't time that was wasted. For five years, I was taught Mystical Theology by my mentor and others like him that I followed at an academic level. Life is about learning, unlearning, and relearning. The earlier we understand this, the better.

When I initially started my master's, I couldn't fund it. When I wanted to go to school to do my certification as a copy editor, I literally couldn't afford it. God opened up opportunities for me as a businessman that completely blew my mind. I was able to do my copy-editing course and restart my master's affordably. As a matter of fact, the school allowed me to pick up where I left off after eight years, which I believe is a miracle in itself.

Faith is not a standalone technology. It doesn't just produce because we want it to. Faith is acting on what God has said, so hearing His voice is paramount to walking in great faith. The centurion said he understood authority, and Jesus only needed to **"say the words."**

When the Lord told me to write plays and sell them online, initially, I had no idea what I was doing. God provided a mentor until I could stand on my own two feet. When the Lord told me to write and publish my first book, I had no idea how to do that. God provided mentors and resources that propelled me into the business of book publishing at the highest possible level. No one to date has been able to replicate the value and quality of publishing and writing services I have been able to provide to my clients. We exercise great faith by believing what God has said.

I will worship toward Your holy temple and praise Your name for Your lovingkindness and Your truth; for You have magnified Your word above all Your name. (Psalm 138:2 - NKJV).

Then the Lord said to me, "You have seen well, for I am ready to perform My word." (Jeremiah 1:12 - NKJV).

The challenge facing us is to believe God, obey His Word, and experience the manifestation of what is spoken.

CHAPTER 18

PERFECT LOVE: THE FOUNDATION OF SUPERNATURAL FAITH

We cannot discuss faith without talking about love because both are intricately connected. Perfect love is not just an abstract ideal, it is the very essence of God's nature and the cornerstone of a vibrant, faith-filled life. In a world that often seems fragmented and divisive, the call to love one another as Christ loves us is both a radical and transformative command. Without love, our acts of faith will not bear fruit. Loving others is the single greatest commandment Jesus gives to us, and it is the prerequisite for walking in the supernatural and witnessing miracles.

When asked about the greatest commandment, Jesus answered unequivocally in Matthew 22:37-39 (The Message), **"'Love the Lord your God with all your passion and prayer and intelligence.' This is the most important, the first on any list. But there is a second to set alongside it: 'Love others as well as you love yourself.'"** These commandments are inextricably linked;

loving God with all our being naturally flows into loving others. This love is not a superficial feeling but a selfless act that mirrors God's unconditional love for us. Faith without love is hollow and ineffective. In Galatians 5:6 (The Passion Translation), Paul writes, **"When you're placed into the Anointed One and joined to him, circumcision and religious obligations can benefit you nothing. All that matters now is living in the faith that is activated and brought to perfection by love."** This verse illuminates that faith is not merely a belief but is energized and perfected through love. Without love, faith lacks the substance and power to manifest the supernatural.

The ministry of Jesus exemplifies how love and the supernatural are intertwined. Every miracle He performed was an act of compassion and love. When Jesus fed the five thousand, healed the sick, or raised the dead, it was always rooted in a deep love for humanity. In John 13:34-35 (The Message), Jesus says, **"Let me give you a new command: Love one another. In the same way I loved you, you love one another. This is how everyone will recognize that you are my disciples—when they see the love you have for each other."** This love is the hallmark of true discipleship and the conduit for God's miraculous power. Unity within the ecclesia (the called-out assembly or church) is essential for rising in power. Ephesians 4:2-3 (The Passion Translation) urges, **"With tender humility and quiet patience, always demonstrate gentleness and generous love toward one another, especially toward those who may try your patience. Be faithful to guard the sweet**

harmony of the Holy Spirit among you in the bonds of peace." True unity is achieved when we love one another despite our differences, reflecting the unity of the Spirit and creating an environment where the supernatural can thrive.

Perfect love is inclusive, extending even to those who oppose or differ from us. Jesus' teaching in Matthew 5:44-45 (The Message) is revolutionary: **"I'm telling you to love your enemies. Let them bring out the best in you, not the worst. When someone gives you a hard time, respond with the energies of prayer, for then you are working out of your true selves, your God-created selves."** This command to love our enemies challenges us to move beyond our natural inclinations and embrace a divine perspective, seeing others through the eyes of grace and compassion. God's love towards a fallen humanity is the ultimate example of perfect love. Romans 5:8 (The Passion Translation) states, **"But Christ proved God's passionate love for us by dying in our place while we were still lost and ungodly!"** This sacrificial love is not based on our merit but on God's nature. As recipients of such love, we are called to extend the same grace to others, regardless of their beliefs or actions.

The early church exemplified the power of love in community. Acts 2:44-47 (The Message) describes, **"All the believers lived in a wonderful harmony, holding everything in common... They followed a daily discipline of worship in the Temple followed by meals at home, every meal a celebration, exuberant and joyful, as they**

praised God. People in general liked what they saw. Every day their number grew as God added those who were saved." This harmonious and loving community was a powerful witness to the world, attracting others to the faith and facilitating the outpouring of the Holy Spirit. Walking in the supernatural is intrinsically linked to walking in love. 1 Corinthians 13:1-2 (The Passion Translation) poignantly reminds us, **"If I were to speak with eloquence in earth's many languages, and in the heavenly tongues of angels, yet I didn't express myself with love, my words would be reduced to the hollow sound of nothing more than a clanging cymbal... I am nothing without love."** The supernatural gifts of the Spirit are given for the purpose of edifying the body of Christ and demonstrating God's love to the world. Without love, these gifts become meaningless and ineffective.

As we live out our walk of faith, we must learn to love, and to love beyond even the faults of others. I have written extensively on this topic in other books, so I won't belabor the point, but we must recognize that perfect love does not mean it flows from perfection. It means that despite our flaws and shortcomings, we have this intrinsic capacity to extend love, even to the underserving. This opens up the portals of heaven over our lives, and causes the culture of the world where we were born to flow through and out into this world where we were formed. As 1 John 4:12 (The Message) beautifully puts it, **"No one has seen God, ever. But if we love one another, God dwells deeply within us, and his love becomes complete in us—perfect love!"**

CHAPTER 19

TRUSTING GOD

In an age where humanity prides itself on independence and self-sufficiency, the concept of trusting God can seem antiquated or even irrelevant. Our modern world is brimming with advanced systems designed to function independently of divine intervention. From medical breakthroughs to financial markets, from social networks to technological innovations, we have built a society that mirrors the ancient Tower of Babel, where humans came together to create a name for themselves, forgetting the one who holds the name above all names. As believers, how do we navigate this reality to restore the level of trust in God exemplified by Biblical writers? Faith, at its core, is about trusting God above all else.

The story of the Tower of Babel (see Genesis 11:1-9) is a fitting example of humanity's attempt to assert independence from God. The people of Babel sought to build a tower that reached the heavens, making a name for themselves and preventing their dispersion across the earth. Their endeavor was marked by a collective confidence in human ingenuity and effort, sidelining the need for divine guidance or approval. They would have succeeded had God not intervened. God responded by confusing their language and scattering them, disrupting their plans and reminding them of their dependence on Him.

This narrative is a powerful allegory for our times. In our pursuit of progress and security, we often place our trust in human capabilities, technologies, and institutions. While these advancements are not inherently wrong, the danger lies in the attitude of self-reliance that neglects our need for God. Just as the people of Babel sought to build their own destiny apart from God, we too can fall into the trap of trusting in our systems more than in our Creator.

Today's culture promotes the virtues of independence, self-reliance, and do-it-yourself (DIY) mentality. From a young age, we are taught to forge our own paths, solve our own problems, and find our own way. This cultural narrative can make trusting God seem counterintuitive. After all, why rely on an unseen deity when we have the tools and knowledge to manage our lives? However, the Biblical perspective challenges this mindset. Proverbs 3:5-6 (The Message) urges us to, **"Trust God from the bottom of your heart; don't try to figure out everything on your own. Listen for God's voice in everything you do, everywhere you go; he's the one who will keep you on track."** This passage emphasizes the futility of leaning solely on our understanding and the importance of seeking God's guidance in every aspect of our lives.

One of the most compelling aspects of Biblical faith is the ability to trust God in the face of uncertainty. The Biblical writers often found themselves in situations where human solutions were insufficient, and trusting God was their only recourse. Consider Abraham, who trusted God's promise of a son despite his and Sarah's advanced age (see Romans 4:18-21). Or consider Moses, who led the Israelites out of Egypt, trusting God to part the Red Sea and provide manna in the wilderness (see Exodus 14:21-22, 16:4-5). These stories are not just historical accounts but testimonies of faith that goes beyond human logic and limitations. They remind us that trusting God often means stepping out in faith, even when the outcome is uncertain or seems impossible. Hebrews 11:1 (The Passion Translation) defines faith as **"the assurance of what we hope for and the certainty of what we do not see."** This kind of faith requires a deep-seated trust in God's character and promises, regardless of our circumstances.

Trusting God begins with a daily decision to surrender our plans, fears, and desires to Him. This act of surrender is not a one-time event but a continual process of yielding our will to God's. Jesus modeled this in the Garden of Gethsemane, praying, **"Not my will, but yours be done"** (Luke 22:42 - The Message). By starting each day with a prayer of surrender, we acknowledge our dependence on God and invite Him to guide our steps.

Faith comes from hearing the Word of God (see Romans 10:17). Immersing ourselves in Scripture helps us understand God's nature, promises, and past faithfulness. As we read about God's interactions with His people, our trust in Him deepens. Scripture also provides wisdom and direction for our daily lives, helping us navigate challenges with a God-centered perspective. Additionally, prayer is our lifeline to God. It is through prayer that we communicate our needs, fears, and desires to Him. More importantly, prayer is an opportunity to listen to God's voice. Philippians 4:6-7 (The Message) encourages us to **"not fret or worry. Instead of worrying, pray. Let petitions and praises shape your worries into prayers, letting God know your concerns."** Through consistent prayer, we develop a habit of turning to God first, rather than relying on our own solutions.

The ecclesia, or the community of believers, plays a crucial role in fostering trust in God. Hebrews 10:24-25 (The Passion Translation) exhorts us to **"discover creative ways to encourage others and to motivate them toward acts of compassion, doing beautiful works as expressions of love."** Being part of a faith community provides support, encouragement, and accountability. We are reminded that we are not alone on our journey of faith and that we can draw strength from each other. Recalling instances where God has been faithful in the past strengthens our trust in Him for the future. David often reflected on God's past deliverance as he faced new challenges (see Psalm 77:11-12). Keeping a journal of answered prayers and God's interventions in our lives can serve as a tangible reminder of His faithfulness.

Trusting God is not passive; it requires action. James 2:17 (The Message) states, **"Isn't it obvious that God-talk without God-acts is outrageous nonsense?"** Faith without works is dead. When we trust God, we must be willing to act on His guidance, even when it challenges our understanding or comfort. Obedience is the ultimate expression of trust, demonstrating our belief that God's ways are higher than our own.

Despite our best efforts, several barriers can hinder our ability to trust God fully. These include:

- **Fear and Anxiety:** Fear of the unknown and anxiety about the future can paralyze our faith. Jesus addresses this in Matthew 6:25-34, urging us not to worry about our lives but to seek God's kingdom first. Trusting God requires us to cast our anxieties on Him, believing that He cares for us (see 1 Peter 5:7).

- **Past Disappointments:** Unmet expectations and past hurts can erode our trust in God. It is essential to process these disappointments with God, seeking healing and understanding. Proverbs 3:5 (The Passion Translation) reminds us to **"trust in the Lord completely, and do not rely on your own opinions."** God's perspective often transcends our understanding, and He can bring good out of even the most painful experiences (see Romans 8:28).

- **Self-Reliance:** Our culture of independence can make it challenging to relinquish control to God. We must recognize that true strength lies in acknowledging our weakness and dependence on Him. Paul writes in 2 Corinthians 12:9 (The Passion Translation), **"But he answered me, 'My grace is always more than enough for you, and my power finds its full expression through your weakness.'"**

- **Cultural Pressures:** The world often promotes values that are contrary to Biblical principles, making it difficult to trust God. We must be vigilant in guarding our hearts and minds, allowing God's Word to shape our beliefs and actions rather than societal norms (see Romans 12:2).

I beseech you therefore, brethren, by the mercies of God, that you present your bodies a living sacrifice, holy, acceptable to God, which is your reasonable service. And do not be conformed to this world, but be transformed by the renewing of your mind, that you may prove what is that good and acceptable and perfect will of God. (Romans 12:1-2 - NKJV).

Trusting God in a world that emphasizes self-sufficiency and independence is undoubtedly challenging but not impossible. We can develop a deeper trust in God by surrendering daily, immersing ourselves in Scripture, cultivating a prayer life, engaging with a faith community, reflecting on God's past faithfulness, and acting in obedience. In this modern age, let us remember that true faith involves trusting God above all else. Just as the Biblical writers leaned on God amidst their trials, we too can find strength and guidance in Him. Trusting God is not about abandoning reason or effort but about recognizing our limitations and placing our ultimate hope in His infinite wisdom and love.

Recently, I had the privilege to study books one and two of Adam and Eve. These books are included in the Lost Books of the Bible and were not canonized. This is not a campaign to gain consideration for their inclusion, but there are lessons to learn from even those **"historical"** documents. Adam and Eve were created perfect in a perfect world. In terms of consciousness, they were as God-conscious as a human being can get. Yet, they made a bad choice. What is remarkable is that they fell prey to the voice of a creature that promised them things it had no means to fulfill. Satan wanted to give Adam and Eve something he desired for himself but couldn't attain. Thus, humanity fell.

As I study Scripture, I am fascinated by the clarity with which Adam and Eve, in their fallen state, and Cain, who became a murderous vagabond, were able to communicate with God. That clarity seems to be missing today, even among those who claim to be **"prophetic."** Comparing then and now can prove burdensome when the answers are not readily available. However, one of my lecturers in a recent course I completed said of Enoch that **"walking with God"** is the answer to death. I appreciate this conclusion because it is biblically sound. The concept that one can live and not die is something the church has tiptoed around for years, adhering only to the reality that we all **"die once."** Reflecting on the fall of man from the canon and other writings, I realize that we have descended to a very low place where even the voice of God has lost its clarity. We have embraced a culture of self-sufficiency to the point where we do not consult God before making decisions. This, for me, is a very sad reality because we have learned to navigate life and church without God while simultaneously attaching His name to what we do to create some semblance of validity.

I emphasize faith and trust because if this world is to change, there must be a restoration of our capacity to walk with God and in God. We must relearn our total dependency on Him to the point where we do nothing without first consulting Him. This is a lost culture in our day, but I believe a generation will arise, as it was in the days of Seth, when people began to call on the name of the Lord again. Despite our modernization and self-aggrandizing culture, we can usher in an age where people once again place all their hope, trust, and faith in God, our Creator and Abba. This is the clarion call for this generation and generations to come. Will you answer that call?

May we, the ecclesia, rise in faith, trusting God with the same fervor and conviction as the saints of old, and may our lives be a testament to His enduring faithfulness and grace.

CHAPTER 20

FAITH OF A MYSTIC

There are people around me who never grasp my choice to pursue mystical theology. It was not a journey I chose for myself, but one that the Lord led me to and that I eventually embraced. It was not easy at first because of my strong religious background. I had to overcome my own reservations to sit under over 150 hours of teaching each year for over five years. What I learned on that journey is that the spiritual side of Christianity, which is often fervently opposed by conservative Christians, addresses the inner structure of the believer.

Religion tends to focus on the outer aspects of the believer like the outer courts of a temple. I finally understood what Jesus was talking about:

"Woe to you, scribes and Pharisees, hypocrites! For you cleanse the outside of the cup and dish, but inside they are full of extortion and self-indulgence. Blind Pharisee, first cleanse the inside of the cup and dish, that the

outside of them may be clean also." (Matthew 23:25-26 – NKJV).

Christianity as a religion often emphasizes external transformation through rules and laws, yet within, there may be little real change or transformation. The consequence of this can be clergy struggling with issues like homosexuality and adultery, never finding the true freedom of being a child of God. Our struggles often reflect our level of spiritual maturity.

"A child falters and needs correction, but a son does not sin. Whoever has been born of God does not sin, for His seed remains in him; and he cannot sin, because he has been born of God." (1 John 3:9 - NKJV).

One issue I encountered growing up in church is that it can foster an environment of pretense. I recall being in a youth service where everyone started acting **"crazy"** in the spirit. I don't particularly object to how people respond to the Spirit's leading, but personally, I am not inclined to such behavior, at least not in that manner. It is not that I am unwilling to participate, but rather I choose not to pretend. My decision to remain a passive observer earned me a physical **"beating"** with a Bible. Yes, evangelical Protestants can do some peculiar things. The judgment was that my lack of response indicated a problem that needed addressing.

When we elevate a believer who has climbed the ranks to become a bishop, with an outward appearance of transformation but an immature inner life, it forces many to silently struggle while presenting a religious and seemingly mature facade. Often, we are the ones who place such individuals on pedestals, define their expectations, and then we are also the ones who bring them down. We tend to hold those with titles like Bishop, Prophet, Apostle, etc., to higher standards than the average person, yet when they struggle with internal issues, they often keep these hidden. This dynamic contributes to the scandals that frequently emerge involving people of high religious authority.

Mystical theology focuses on our union with Christ and the transformation that results from pursuing that reality. It emphasizes change from the inside out, which is the only genuine path to maturity as a child of God, and that is what I desire above all else.

It is okay to be different. If your path takes you down a road less travelled, don't be burdened by those who would impose their own expectations on you about who you are and what you should be doing. My encouragement to young people today is to believe in yourself. Don't buy into the rubbish that is often projected onto you by others. What matters most is what you believe about yourself, and the choice is yours: **to believe what is true about you or to believe the lies.** If we embrace the lies, we will never transcend our limitations. We were created to overcome this world so that a greater glory than the effects of the fall can be revealed in and through us. That is the journey you are on, and it is an expedition of faith. The thesaurus reveals some negative connotations for the word **"mystic,"** but that is just the nature of the world we live in today. A true mystic is one who pursues the heart and mind of God, who seeks to experience Him and not just know about Him. A true mystic interacts with angels, not demons, and has experiential knowledge of the unseen realm through dreams, prophetic infusion, etc. Every Christian should be a mystic.

There are too many churchgoers and passive observers in the ecclesia. God is searching for those who will participate and partner with Him in what He wants to do. The alternative is to pursue our own fantasies and do **"whatever we think is right in our own eyes."** As we draw nearer to the close of this book, I declare that your faith will be active. I declare that your capacity to hear God's voice with clarity will increase, and you will have the heart and tenacity to obey His voice. Great faith will arise in your heart to see the impossible manifest before your very eyes. The mystical/spiritual realm of God and all its mysteries will open up to you, and you will begin to see and interact with angels and understand your true identity in God. And if you ever find yourself alone on your faith walk, may I remind you that you are in good company:

"But you have come to Mount Zion and to the city of the living God, the heavenly Jerusalem, to an innumerable company of angels, to the general assembly and church of the firstborn who are registered in heaven, to God the

Judge of all, to the spirits of just men made perfect, to Jesus the Mediator of the new covenant, and to the blood of sprinkling that speaks better things than that of Abel." (Hebrews 12:22-24 - NKJV).

CHAPTER 21

UNITY AMONG DIVERSITY

God is Source and sits at the very foundation of all things created. What we see and experience about the world and ourselves was first a thought in the mind of God, and it all exists in God. God is as much unique as He is a mystery, and what is known about Him is what He has chosen to reveal. *"If God is unique, it follows logically that He does not resemble His creatures, neither in essence, nor in attributes nor in actions."* (Tennant, 35). In examining the reality of His existence, there are two things that must be discussed: His oneness and His plurality. *"Islam, Judaism and Christianity all affirm that God is One. This is the most basic shared predicate of all monotheists. Judaism along with Christianity wholeheardtedly affirms the Shema, "Hear, O Israel, The Lord our God, the Lord is one." (Deut. 6:4)."* (Tennant, 40).

Most theologians accept that the Bible reveals God's oneness before His three-ness, but I submit that the plurality of God was evident from the very beginning. The Bible states, **"In the beginning God created the heaven and the**

earth." (Genesis 1:1 - KJV). That is about all the introduction we get to this Deity just prior to creation emerging from His mind through the Spirit hovering over a very chaotic scene, and the Word spoken to create. **And God said, Let there be light: and there was light. (Genesis 1:3 - KJV).** The only logical conclusion we can draw from this very vague introduction is that God has always existed, even before there was a beginning. It means then that the **"beginning"** originated in Him, and He dwells in a realm outside of time itself. It is hard for the human mind to comprehend a living Being who has no beginning or end.

The first mystery that scripture reveals about God was when He spoke regarding the creation of man, **"And God said, Let us make man in our image, after our likeness:" (Genesis 1:26 - KJV).** The use of the word **"US"** signifies that God, the self-existing one who has no beginning or end and is not subjected to time, space or matter, was not alone. We see the plurality of God suggested from the very first chapter of the Bible. I have contemplated the idea of **'God'** from the very first Chapter of the Bible, **"Let US make man..."** If in the beginning, **"God"** was present, then who was there with Him?

And the earth was without form, and void; and darkness was upon the face of the deep. And the Spirit of God moved upon the face of the waters. (Genesis 1:2 - KJV).

The Spirit of God was present before the beginning.

In the beginning was the Word, and the Word was with God, and the Word was God. (John 1:1 - KJV).

The Word of God was present in the beginning. Was this a being or a person?

And the Word was made flesh, and dwelt among us, (and we beheld his glory, the glory as of the only begotten of the Father,) full of grace and truth. (John 1:14 - KJV).

The Son of God was present in the beginning but in a different form. He was not yet flesh. There was one other being present in the beginning, according to Scripture. In speaking about Wisdom, Solomon wrote:

The Lord possessed me at the beginning of His way, before His works of old. I have been established from everlasting, from the beginning, before there was ever an earth. (Proverbs 8:22-23 - NKJV).

Within God, there is a **'Us'** from the very beginning. Wisdom was present in the beginning but not included in the Godhead. According to Dr. Fairbairn, the Trinity is a very complicated theological claim about God's existence. Yet, it speaks to the pattern of God's revelation in Scripture about Himself.

I have never doubted the revelation of the Trinity, even though I struggled to comprehend it. It is obvious in

Scripture that God is one, though three distinct persons **(Father, Son, and Holy Spirit).** This is my personal belief. I usually use man as an example of this. We are body, soul and spirit, but one person. God is Father, Son and Holy Spirit, but one God. Even with that knowledge, it is still hard to fathom the mystery of it all.

One scripture was brought to light that made me grasp this even more. **"For in him dwelleth all the fulness of the Godhead bodily." (Colossians 2:9 - KJV).** In Christ, the fullness of the Father, Son and Holy Spirit dwells bodily. We could say in the Holy Spirit, the fullness of the Godhead dwells. In the Father, the fullness of the Godhead dwells. So, I surmise that we may never see all three standing side by side as our imagination often interprets this mystery when trying to conjure up an imagery. If we see Jesus, we see all three. If we see Holy Spirit, we see all three. If we see the Father, we see all three. Never separate, but always one. Based on what I have learned, this would be my basic understanding of the Trinity.

The temptation is always trying to grasp infinite mystery with a finite mind and limited imagination. We try to understand by wrapping our mortal minds around a concept that may be much bigger than we can possibly grasp, and I think this is why without faith, we cannot please God. We may not be able to comprehend God to act, but we are not admonished to understand God, only to have faith. We can believe without understanding or comprehending. If we try to use our present grid of what we know to grasp the doctrine of the Trinity, it will get utterly confusing. One of the most profound prayers of Jesus recorded in Scripture is in John 17.

I do not pray for these alone, but also for those who will believe in Me through their word; that they all may be one, as You, Father, are in Me, and I in You; that they also may be one in Us, that the world may believe that You sent Me. (John 17:20-21 - NKJV).

The idea of **"oneness"** is a beautiful thing, and a mystery for the most part. I think when the church finally grasps the reality of God's oneness, though three, then we can start to talk about how we participate in that, because I don't think we know the full extent of our **"partaking of God's divine nature."** This is where I may disagree with some theological conclusions, but it is a conversation I am sure will keep reoccurring in the future.

God is one, but three. No separation. We are one with God, but separate (Ref. Jesus' prayer in John 17).

Jesus said He did not come to do His own will, but that of the Father. When it was time for Him to leave, He said the Holy Spirit will come and He will not speak on His own authority but that which He hears, He will speak. So even though we see the Trinity as three but one, there is an aspect of the Trinity where only that which the Father wills is mandatory. Neither Jesus nor the Holy Spirit acts on their own will. Even within the Godhead, there is a surrender of wills, where only that of the Father truly matters. Even though in the beginning we know there was God but a **"Us",** I believe this alludes to the possibility that while there is a **"Us"** that is separated from God, in the end, we may learn that there was really just **"God."**

As we progress through Scripture in our understanding of who God is, we begin to learn His character and attributes through revelations of His **"Names"** as the central mode through which God has revealed Himself to humanity. This was necessary throughout history so that we could differentiate God from all other **"entities."** The world is much bigger than our limited purview.

The first name we encounter in scripture is Elohim (see Genesis 1:1, Isaiah 54:5, Jeremiah 32:27, Isaiah 45:18, Deuteronomy 5:23, 8:15, Psalm 68:7). Elohim: The plural form of EL, meaning **"strong one."** It is used of false gods, but when used of the true God, it is a plural of majesty and intimates the trinity. It is especially used of God's sovereignty, creative work, mighty work for Israel, and in relation to His sovereignty.[11]

We see compounds of El:

- **El Shaddai: "God Almighty."** The derivation is uncertain. Some think it stresses God's loving supply

---

[11] https://bible.org/article/names-god

and comfort; others His power as the Almighty one standing on a mountain and who corrects and chastens (see Genesis 17:1; 28:3; 35:11; Exodus 6:1; Psalm 91:1, 2).

- **El Elyon: "The Most High God."** Stresses God's strength, sovereignty, and supremacy (see Genesis 14:19; Psalm 9:2; Daniel 7:18, 22, 25).

- **El Olam: "The Everlasting God."** Emphasizes God's unchangeableness and is connected with His inexhaustibleness (see Genesis 16:13).[12]

The next name we encounter is Yahweh (YHWH), which derives from a verb which means **"to exist, be."** Its usage shows that this name stresses God as the independent and self-existent God of revelation and redemption (see Genesis 4:3; Exodus 6:3).

This is the name that reveals much of God's character through Scripture and His interactions with different Biblical writers:

- **Yahweh Jireh (Yireh): "The Lord will provide."** God provides for His people (see Genesis 22:14).

---

[12] https://bible.org/article/names-god

- **Yahweh Nissi: "The Lord is my Banner."** God is our rallying point and our means of victory; the one who fights for His people (see Exodus 17:15).

- **Yahweh Shalom: "The Lord is Peace."** The Lord is the means of our peace and rest (see Judges 6:24).

- **Yahweh Sabbaoth: "The Lord of Hosts."** A military figure portraying the Lord as the commander of the armies of heaven (see 1 Samuel 1:3; 17:45).

- **Yahweh Ro'i: "The Lord my Shepherd."** The Lord is the Shepherd who cares for His people as a shepherd cares for the sheep of his pasture (see Psalm 23:1).

- **Yahweh Tsidkenu: "The Lord our Righteousness."** The Lord is our righteousness (see Jeremiah 23:6).

- **Yahweh Shammah: "The Lord is there."** The Lord is present in the millennial kingdom (see Ezekiel 48:35).

- **Yahweh Elohim Israel: "The Lord, the God of Israel."** Identifies Yahweh as the God of Israel in contrast to the false gods of the nations (see Judges 5:3; Isaiah 17:6).

Interestingly, God reveals much of Himself throughout the Old Testament through different names that point to His character and divine attributes. When we get into the New Testament, under the new covenant where the Word of God becomes flesh, here, we see the culmination of all the names in one person:

Wherefore God also hath highly exalted him, and given him a name which is above every name: that at the name of Jesus every knee should bow, of things in heaven, and things in earth, and things under the earth; and that every tongue should confess that Jesus Christ is Lord, to the glory of God the Father. (Philippians 2:9-11 - KJV).

Now there is one name that reveals the Father, and his name is Jesus.

Jesus answered: "Don't you know me, Philip, even after I have been among you such a long time? Anyone who has seen me has seen the Father. How can you say, 'Show us the Father'? (John 14:9 - NIV).

God reveals Himself through His names so we understand His divine attributes and character, and He has fully made Himself known through His Son, Jesus Christ, who is the way, truth, and life. No one can access the Father except through the Son, and no one can access the Son except the Holy Spirit draws them.

As a writer, which I believe is my core ministry, I have an opportunity to explore many different levels of theological discussions. In my country, we have an apostolic movement (body of churches) that we call **"Jesus only."** They believe that the Father is Jesus, the Son is Jesus, and the Holy Spirit is Jesus. I don't believe the Bible supports this theology. I believe in God as three persons who constitute one God. This understanding helps me to celebrate the uniqueness of individuals without compromising the need and necessity for unity in the body of Christ. We can be as unique as each person in the Godhead but still function as one unit: as one body with many members. Our differences are not a hindrance to unity but our unique contribution to the whole. In other words, you have something to offer, and you have a place in the kingdom of God. Your faith, your life, the very essence of your being is a part of the whole.

CHAPTER 22

UNDERSTANDING WHO WE ARE IN CHRIST

I have gone through a process to get to where I am today. It was not easy, and every step of the way required faith. To fully grasp what I have shared in this theological memoir, you must understand my background. I grew up with both my parents, but I don't recall having the kind of close, sit-down conversations with them. In my twenties, I asked my mother why she never talked to me about sex. Her reply was, **"Didn't you have guidance counselors at school?"** If I did, I wouldn't have understood their role in educating me about life.

I have shared some negative things my father said while I was growing up, which had an adverse effect on my psyche. But I don't want you to think it was all negative. I also remember many moments of laughter when he shared **"duppy"** stories with us. To this day, I don't know if some of the crazy tales he told were true. I remember him buying us ice cream, cornflakes and milk, and Chinese patties. I remember him taking us to Salt River early Sunday mornings before we got ready for church. I also recall several company functions where he took me, and I fell in love with roast fish and got to taste some unique **"delicacies"** like turtle skin soap. It wasn't all bad, but I was never fully exposed enough to mature in my thinking and language.

In high school, I was laughed at because of my thick Jamaican accent. To this day, I cannot shake the potency of my dialect when I speak, even when I try to use the Queen's English. When I started to travel, I often had to repeat myself to be understood. I was also extremely shy and found it difficult to make friends or speak up, earning me the nickname **"the quiet one."** Even when asked to do simple tasks at church, like reading the Bible, I would tremble so hard that my voice shook, making it evident I was nervous. I was the guy who preferred to stay behind the scenes at church, avoiding being called upon because it would shake my nerves to the core. I once told my men's director that all I could do was read a scripture; I wasn't willing or able to do anything else. But this was a lie I had convinced myself of entirely.

God has brought me a long way. I have hosted three international conferences in Jamaica with my mentor, who travels the world preaching the gospel and teaching about the kingdom and sonship on a global scale. I have traveled a lot—maybe too much—been on a cruise, and seen my name in print in many different countries. I have created an impact that I may never fully know in this life. My writings have touched many people. I have preached, taught Bible studies, and started an online ministry where I taught a weekly Bible study for a full year. I don't know how God did it, but I am more convinced now that who we think we are is not the end of the story. If God did it for me, He will do it for you.

At the beginning of 2024, the Lord gave me one word: **Faith.** That was the only word I carried throughout the year. Everything I did revolved around that word. It was a profound learning experience for me. I haven't yet seen what faith can accomplish at epic biblical proportions, but I believe. I know there is more to our **"reality"** than meets the eye, and I am committed to the long haul.

As a student of theology, I recognize that theology has evolved. We are discussing topics now that theology did not address twenty years ago, and it is crucial to understand that I am a theologian, though an apparently controversial one. You can't write 49 books without being one. Since my early twenties, I have been studying theology wherever I could find it. I have always had a hunger for knowledge. God, for me, remains the greatest mystery because He hides Himself to reveal Himself to those who seek Him.

The second greatest mystery for me is women, but that's a topic for another book.

In studying theology, I realize there is freedom in formulating our own theological ideas. I now understand the importance of knowing what we believe and being able to articulate it. I have been delivered from trying to emulate others. This began my journey with the core idea that *"Faith Without Works Is Dead."* To that, I add **"Works Without Love Is Fruitless."** Every serious student of Scripture has a foundational idea that shapes their beliefs, whether they realize it or not.

"Who Am I in Christ" is my lifelong theme. I can never exhaust exploring it because it is tied to our origins when humanity was created in the image and likeness of God. It is a position we lost but have yet to fully experience in its restoration. We still live in an era where born-again believers don't believe they can do what Jesus did. Yet, this is the foundation of faith.

When I met my wife, one of the activities we did while courting was enrolling in the Leadership Development Institute, the theological arm of our denomination. It was there we met Rev. Andrew Green. Before we got married, his wedding gift to us was marital counseling and a deliverance session. During our first counseling session, he asked me, ***"Who are you in Christ?"*** I thought I knew the answer—I was saved, sanctified, and filled with the Holy Ghost—but that wasn't the answer. This started me on a journey to discover my identity in Christ, which profoundly impacted my life.

Let me clarify that as a believer in Christ, you are not ordinary. Sometimes, I hesitate to use the word **"Christian"** because I believe it has been overly commercialized and misused. A Christian is not just someone who attends church; a Christian is someone who believes in Jesus. I want to challenge our faith today to believe God, especially with what I am about to reveal regarding your identity.

There are Christians who don't believe in God but love going to church. I believe a time is coming when believers will choose either to embrace a mystical/supernatural reality of Christianity or become atheists. The problem with Christianity isn't a lack of evidence but an identity crisis. We have no idea who we are.

Then God said, "Let Us make man in Our image, according to Our likeness; let them have dominion over the fish of the sea, over the birds of the air, and over the cattle, over all the earth and over every creeping thing that creeps on the earth." (Genesis 1:26 – NKJV).

And the LORD God formed man of the dust of the ground, and breathed into his nostrils the breath of life; and man became a living soul. (Genesis 2:6 – KJV).

God spoke creation into being, but man He formed. Thus, the fingerprint of God is embedded in man. Man also became a **"living soul."** I believe the soul is more than just the seat of our will, intellect, and emotions. I believe the soul is a spiritual body within our physical body, and it represents the real, eternal us, until our bodies are changed. Though I am fine with referring to this as the **"Spirit Man,"** I want to make that distinction because it is key to understanding our identity in Christ.

"Behold, all souls are mine; as the soul of the father, so also the soul of the son is mine: the soul that sinneth, it shall die." (Ezekiel 18:4 – KJV).

The moment Eve ate that fruit, she was no longer a living soul; her soul died immediately. My theology holds that unbelievers have a dead soul. They are born dead in trespasses and sin. Faith in God, even before Jesus came, activated something in humanity—something that brought forth life. So, when a believer gives their life to Jesus, a new baby soul is born within God, and all the angels in heaven witness this.

"Likewise, I say unto you, there is joy in the presence of the angels of God over one sinner that repenteth." (Luke 15:10 – KJV).

This new soul descends from within God, penetrating your body, shattering the dead soul you once were, and creating a new you. God takes your entire being and places you in Christ.

"But ye are not in the flesh, but in the Spirit, if so be that the Spirit of God dwell in you. Now if any man have not the Spirit of Christ, he is none of his." (Romans 8:9 – KJV).

"Therefore if any man be in Christ, he is a new creature: old things are passed away; behold, all things are become new." (2 Corinthians 5:17 – KJV).

The first time I read that, I was confused. The night I got baptized, I went home with my arm around a girl and my hand on her breast. My mind was still the same. My body and all its desires were still the same. ***So, God, what part of me is new?*** But I was a new soul, born from God, born of God, born in God; completely new, not refurbished, not renewed—I was new. That means whoever the world saw and knew before no longer existed.

As a new baby soul, I needed to grow up, to mature. This isn't achieved only through church attendance or holding church positions. It is accomplished through knowledge (learning) and spiritual practices.

One of the most asked questions in church is, ***"Why are we not seeing the supernatural like in the early church?"*** I have spent many hours probing this question. Let's briefly examine some of the things I have found:

"And they continued stedfastly in the apostles' doctrine and fellowship, and in breaking of bread, and in prayers." (Acts 2:42 – KJV).

We need to return to the practice of daily communion.

"On the morrow, as they went on their journey, and drew nigh unto the city, Peter went up upon the housetop to pray about the sixth hour: And he became very hungry, and would have eaten: but while they made ready, he fell into a trance, and saw heaven opened, and a certain vessel descending upon him, as it had been a great sheet knit at the four corners, and let down to the earth." (Acts 10:9-11 - KJV).

We need to practice prayer, meditation, and fasting. You cannot experience altered states of consciousness without practicing meditation. Notice also the Bible refers to the ninth hour and the sixth hour—these are all times of prayer:

"Now Peter and John went up together into the temple at the hour of prayer, being the ninth hour. And a certain man lame from his mother's womb was carried, whom they laid daily at the gate of the temple which is called Beautiful, to ask alms of them that entered into the temple; Who seeing Peter and John about to go into the temple asked an alms. And Peter, fastening his eyes upon him with John, said, Look on us. And he gave heed unto them, expecting to receive something of them. Then Peter said, Silver and gold have I none; but such as I have give I thee: In the name of Jesus Christ of Nazareth rise up and walk." (Acts 3:1-6 - KJV).

If we are to do what Peter and John did, we need to have what Peter and John had. Faith is a practice, and it goes hand in hand with love.

"Jesus answered and said unto him, if a man love me, he will keep my words: and my Father will love him, and we will come unto him, and make our abode with him." (John 14:23 – KJV).

"And thou shalt love the Lord thy God with all thy heart, and with all thy soul, and with all thy mind, and with all thy strength: this is the first commandment. And the second is like, namely this, Thou shalt love thy neighbour as thyself. There is none other commandment greater than these." (Mark 12:30-31 - KJV).

"If anyone says, "I love God," and hates (works against) his [Christian] brother he is a liar; for the one who does not love his brother whom he has seen, cannot love God whom he has not seen." (1 John 4:20 - AMP).

"This is My commandment, that you love and unselfishly seek the best for one another, just as I have loved you." (John 15:12).

I hope you didn't miss that. God has condensed all 613 commandments into one: **Love one another.** Love is the true sign of Christian maturity and the portal that opens up the heavens over a church. There is no true active faith without love.

"I am giving you a new commandment, that you love one another. Just as I have loved you, so you too are to love one another. By this everyone will know that you are My disciples, if you have love and unselfish concern for one another." (John 13:34-35).

When we reach this place, the Bible says:

"And whatever you ask in My name, that I will do, that the Father may be glorified in the Son. If you ask anything in My name, I will do it." (John 14:13-14 – NKJV).

At this level, when you ask for anything, there are no ulterior motives. I have asked God for many things in His name, and nothing has happened. Confused, I questioned God, and the answer is always the same: **It is a matter of maturity**, and maturity comes when we begin to embrace our identity in Christ.

Understand this: when God placed you into Christ, you became a partaker not only of His divine life but also of the powers of the worlds to come.

We were all in the loins of Adam when he fell, so we all fell. But when the second Adam appeared, everything turned around:

- For when Christ suffered, you suffered.
- When Christ was pierced, you were pierced.
- When Christ was spat upon, you were spat upon.
- When Christ was crucified, you were crucified.
- When Christ was buried, you were buried.
- When Christ was resurrected, you were resurrected.
- When Christ ascended, you ascended.
- So now you are seated with Christ in heavenly places.
- You are made a partaker of God's divine nature.
- You have the power and authority to bring the realities of the world where you were born into this world where you were formed.
- You are a carrier of God's presence.
- You are a temple of the Holy Spirit.
- Nothing is impossible for you.

These statements are eternal, Biblical truths about you. They are forever set in stone and sealed by the blood of Yeshua. You must choose whether to believe them or not. One of the problems with the church is that when we get saved, we are taught to be church members, not disciples. Jesus never said, **"Go into all the world and make church members"**; He said, **"Make disciples."** We were never taught that we carry the power of God within us, which is why so many of our prayers are fruitless—because we keep begging God to come and do things He has empowered us to do.

He gave us His Spirit—the same Spirit that hovered over the chaos in Genesis. He gave us His nature. We have the nature of Christ. We have the mind of Christ. We have the power and authority of Christ. We are the body of Christ in this world. We are the ecclesia. What more do you need?

By your faith, you can lay hands on the sick and see them recover. You will speak in unknown tongues. You will raise the dead back to life. Once you understand your identity and allow God to lead you through the process of maturing your soul, nothing will be impossible.

What does maturity look like?

"Elijah was a man with a nature like ours, and he prayed earnestly that it would not rain; and it did not rain on the land for three years and six months. And he prayed again, and the heaven gave rain, and the earth produced its fruit." (James 5:17-18 – NKJV).

But that's not even my best example:

"Then Joshua spoke to the LORD in the day when the LORD delivered up the Amorites before the children of Israel, and he said in the sight of Israel: 'Sun, stand still over Gibeon; and Moon, in the Valley of Aijalon.' So the

sun stood still, and the moon stopped, till the people had revenge upon their enemies. Is this not written in the Book of Jasher? So the sun stood still in the midst of heaven, and did not hasten to go down for about a whole day." (Joshua 10:12-13 – NKJV).

Now, my memory of science from primary school is a bit vague, but from what I recall, the sun doesn't move. Joshua didn't have access to Google, or he would have known:

> *"The Sun is the center of our solar system, and everything in our solar system revolves around it. This includes the eight planets: Mercury, Venus, Earth, Mars, Jupiter, Saturn, Uranus, and Neptune, as well as asteroids, comets, and space debris. The planets revolve around the Sun in elliptical orbits, with different periods and eccentricities."*

The sun doesn't move. Everything revolves around the sun.

Here is a man who wasn't even in Christ, yet he commanded and halted an entire solar system for a day with his words. We weren't given mouths to gossip, backbite, and curse ourselves and others. I grow weary of hearing believers misuse this power so carelessly. If a man acting in faith can use his mouth to shut up the heavens to stop the rain or halt an entire solar system for a whole day, we need to pay more attention to the power of our words to change our world.

CONCLUSION

As I engaged in a course on Spiritual Formation at the Master's level, one of the points reiterated by the professor is that God is already at work in our lives. Our issue is one of alignment. **Have we aligned ourselves with what He is doing in order to see with clarity how God is already operating in our lives?** This is a big and relevant question we are called upon to answer as people of faith.

As a child of God, our journey is already one of faith. We came into salvation/redemption by faith. We stay saved by faith. The merit of grace is not incumbent on our capacity not to mess up. We mess up. We are flawed on every level. Our own attempts at righteousness only produce filthiness in the eyes of God. Yet, we are called to walk by faith every single day. Everything God allows is a test of our faith, not to give an opportunity for us to fall, but the constant exercising of our faith like a muscle can only strengthen it. Here is something interesting to consider:

And the Lord said, "Simon, Simon! Indeed, Satan has asked for you, that he may sift you as wheat. But I have prayed for you, that your faith should not fail; and when

you have returned to Me, strengthen your brethren." (Luke 22:31-32 - NKJV).

Jesus never prayed a covering over Peter that the devil could not touch him. He prayed that Peter's **"faith should not fail."** This speaks to the value of faith. We may not be spared from the battles we are called upon to fight. We may not avoid some terminal illnesses, debilitating accidents, medical diagnoses, and emergency situations. We may not avoid abuse (sexual, verbal, physical), trauma, loss, or failures on any level. What is most important is that throughout it all, our **"faith should not fail."** Where there is faith, there is hope; where there is hope, there are infinite possibilities of experiencing more favorable outcomes.

Who is he who condemns? It is Christ who died, and furthermore is also risen, who is even at the right hand of God, who also makes intercession for us. (Romans 8:34 - NKJV).

It is the prayer of our Lord and Master that **our faith doesn't fail**, regardless of the circumstances we face in life.

It is my hope and prayer in sharing my story over almost a one-year period that you too will be able to identify the path of faith that has been chosen for you to walk. There are no coincidences in life; every piece of the puzzle is placed there intentionally by divine orientation and serves a greater purpose than just to frustrate you. You already know how the story ends. You have already won. There are many storytellers who start from the end and work their way back to the beginning. This is a good way to view life. The finished product of the process you are going through will be glorious, so do not give up. You win!